MIKAEL KROGERUS AND
ROMAN TSCHÄPPELER

THE COMMUNICATION BOOK

44 IDEAS FOR BETTER CONVERSATIONS EVERY DAY

WITH ILLUSTRATIONS
BY SVEN WEBER

PORTFOLIO
PENGUIN

PORTFOLIO PENGUIN

UK | USA | Canada | Ireland | Australia
India | New Zealand | South Africa

Portfolio Penguin is part of the Penguin Random House group of companies whose addresses can be found at global.penguinrandomhouse.com.

Penguin
Random House
UK

First published as *Das Kommunikationsbuch* by Kein & Aber 2017
This translation published 2018
001

This English translation by Jenny Piening and Lucy Jones is published by kind permission of the Museum für Kommunikation, Bern, Switzerland

Set in 9.5/11.8 pt Rotis Semi Sans
Typeset by Jouve (UK), Milton Keynes
Printed in Great Britain by Clays Ltd, St Ives plc

A CIP catalogue record for this book is available from the British Library

ISBN: 978-0-241-98228-0

www.greenpenguin.co.uk

Penguin Random House is committed to a sustainable future for our business, our readers and our planet. This book is made from Forest Stewardship Council® certified paper.

CONTENTS

Introduction: We Need to Talk

Communication is a bit like love – it's what makes the world go round, but nobody really knows how it works. Communication is something natural, something everyday even, yet most of us have only a vague notion of the rules that govern it. Day in, day out, we ask questions, read, explain, write, listen, argue, discuss or hold our tongues. But only a few of us have the necessary tools to improve the way we communicate or to understand how we're being communicated with. This was the starting point for our exploration of communication theory.

For this book we delved into some of the most important communication theories, assessed their relevance, condensed them, simplified them in the form of diagrams, and applied them to modern-day challenges. We also enhanced them with practical tips and methods. The result: forty-four up-to-date approaches for dealing with eternal problems, from relationships to job interviews, fake news to the filter-bubble effect, small talk to the annual presentation.

This book is actually an exhibition, which came about as follows: the Museum of Communication in Bern, Switzerland, contacted us and asked if we could explain the most important theories in communication history in diagrams. Until 2030 you can experience this book live in the museum.

JOB AND CAREER

1 Six Principle

How to influence

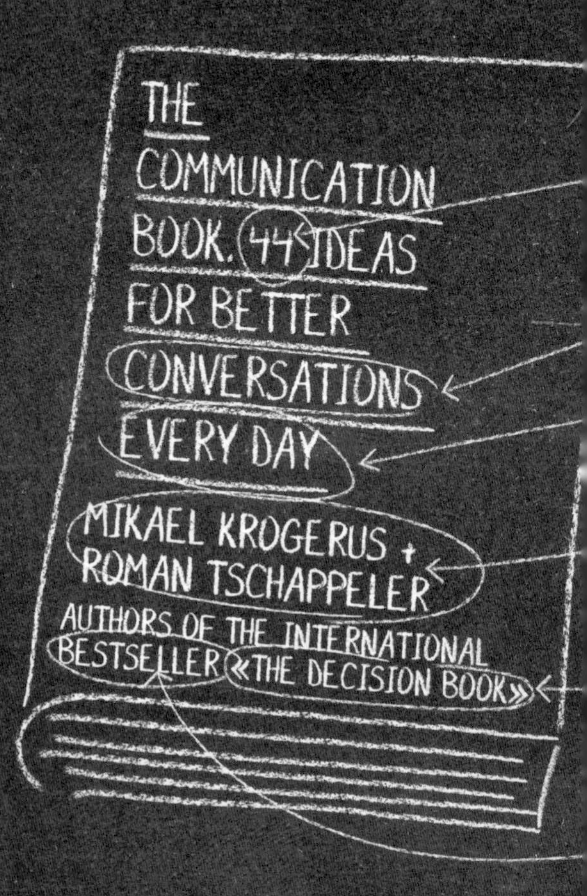

of Persuasion

ople

Robert Cialdini

SCARCITY

RECIPROCITY

CONSISTENCY

LIKING

AUTHORITY

CONSENSUS

How to influence people

An American psychologist, Dr Robert Cialdini, has devoted much of his career to one of the most basic and at the same time biggest questions within communication: when do people say yes? Or more explicitly: can we make them say yes?

Cialdini identified six universal principles that explain how you can persuade someone to accept your suggestion:

1. **Reciprocity**: this is basically the old biblical principle: *Do unto others as you would have them do unto you. Put into action*: if you want to get something, give something. The right order is important: offer something first. Then ask for what you want.
2. **Authority**: we tend to follow the advice of experts. We have more trust in a doctor who is wearing a white coat and displaying diplomas on the wall. *Put into action*: in your area of expertise, find out what the 'white coat' is.
3. **Consistency**: we look up to people who are consistent in their words and behaviours. *Put into action*: stick to one message. Don't follow every trend. Be the consistent one, people will remember you for that.
4. **Consensus**: we are herd people. We do what others do. This is called 'social proof'. *Put into action*: if you want someone to do something, show others doing it ('People who bought this book also bought . . .').

5. **Scarcity**: we all want that which is rare and we are all afraid to lose what we have. *Put into action*: it might not be enough to talk about the benefits of your offer; you also need to point at what people will lose if they fail to act. This also holds true if people face change: they are usually scared of what they might lose. Therefore it's good to tell them what they will lose if they fail to move.
6. **Liking**: this is the most universal principle: people prefer to say yes to people they like. But who do we like? According to Cialdini there are three factors: we like people who are similar to us; we like people who compliment us; we like people who cooperate with us towards a common goal.

'Get in the habit of helping people out, and don't say, "No big deal." Say, "Of course; it's what partners do for each other" – label what happened an act of partnership.'

Robert Cialdini

2 Rules of Mee

Why meetings take

Time available

C. Northcote Parkinson

§ Parkinson's Law

Time you have to accomplish the work

Why meetings take so long

It is one of the great mysteries of the modern world of work: why are meetings so exhausting? And why do they take so long?

According to Seth Godin, there are only three kinds of meetings:

- **Information**: a meeting in which the participants are informed about something (whether they like it or not).
- **Discussion**: a meeting which aims to give input or direction, or to receive feedback.
- **Permission**: a meeting in which one side proposes something, in the hope that the other says yes (but has the right and the power to say no).

What often makes meetings frustrating is the fact that different people might think it's a different kind of meeting. Here are some tips to make meetings run more smoothly:

The fifteen-minute rule

Parkinson's Law states that *Work expands so as to fill the time available for its completion* (and not according to how complex it really is). Therefore it makes sense to limit the time of meetings. Incidentally, studies show that the attention span of the average person is between ten and eighteen minutes. Ideally, you should use a timer. When it rings, the meeting is over – immediately.

The question rule

There are three types of question that you can ask in a meeting: first, comprehension questions; second, questions to support the process (for example, to make sure that everyone has really understood everything and is talking about the same thing); and, third, questions that show how much you know, in order to underscore your own position or challenge another person. All three types of question are legitimate, but they should not be mixed: first come comprehension questions, then questions about the process, then debate questions.

The standing rule

In many companies, meetings are held with everybody standing up because it leads to decisions being reached more quickly (see point 1). At Washington University, studies showed that when they are standing, people react more readily with enthusiasm, whereas when they are sitting, they tend towards scepticism.

The smartphone rule

No smartphones during the meeting. Notes should be made by hand. Even the White House supposedly followed this rule under Barack Obama.

If you want to call a family meeting, just turn off the WiFi router and wait in the room where it is located.

3 Boss Talk

How to talk to (

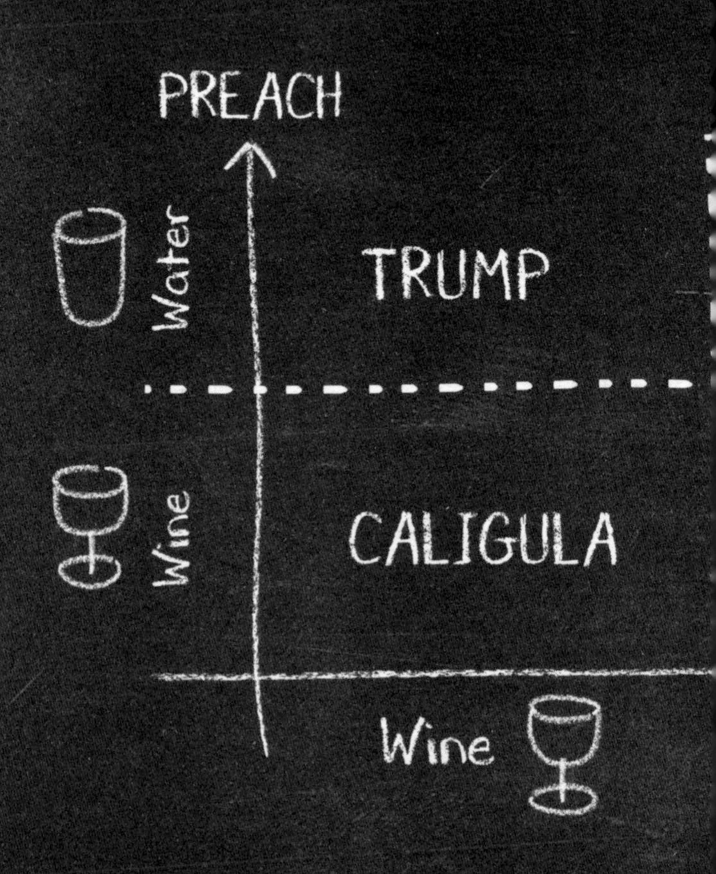

team

GANDHI

SHEEP IN
WOLF'S
CLOTHING

→ PRACTISE

Water

How to talk to your team

Close your eyes for a moment and think about the best boss you ever had. Now think of the worst one. What set them apart?

Most likely, your best boss not only achieved good results, but was also a good communicator. Good bosses get the best out of their employees every day, or at least give them the feeling they are achieving their full potential. But how do they do it? In the context of this book, the question is: How do you communicate properly with your employees, with your team?

Obviously there can't be a universal answer: every person, every situation, every company, every relationship is different. At the same time we all know that we should speak to our team the way we would like to be spoken to: considerately, directly, clearly. We've translated these adverbs into rules.

1. Don't criticize

This might sound a bit too easy-going. And, of course, you have to evaluate the work of your employees – that's your job. But go easy on the criticism. Only start deconstructing if you're prepared to help with the rebuilding. Keep using 'we'. Especially when your team has lost.

2. Give praise (but not too much)

Go easy on the compliments, otherwise they lose their effect. If you celebrate behaviour that you expect, you are lowering standards. Whatever you do, don't give praise simply to please.

3. Practise what you preach

Nothing rings more hollow than words that aren't backed up by deeds. If punctuality and friendliness are important to you, then be punctual and friendly. Set the pace, demonstrate values, establish the tone. But *pick your battles*, only set standards that are important to you – or that you consider to be generally important. You ought to be good at upholding standards that are important to you, and if there are standards that you regard as important but find hard to uphold, then you need to learn them yourself. Share this with your employees. Nobody can be good at everything.

As a leader, get used to the idea that you are primarily responsible for the supply of energy. In other words: motivating, advising, stabilizing, providing momentum – and letting others shine.

4 The Salami

How to carry thr

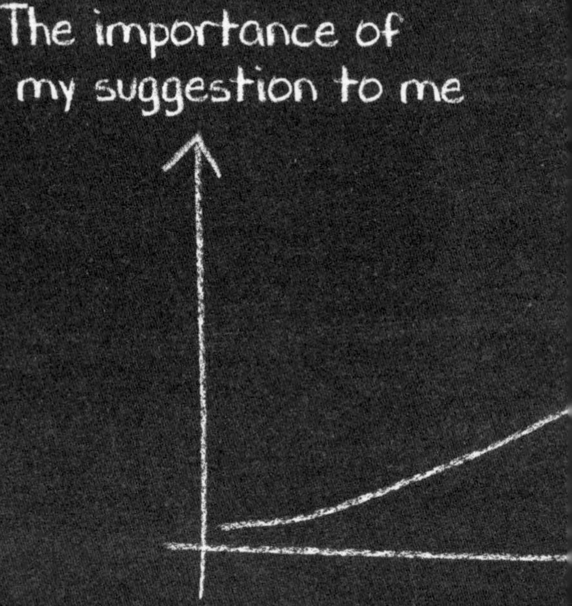

The importance of
my suggestion to me

ctic

h every idea

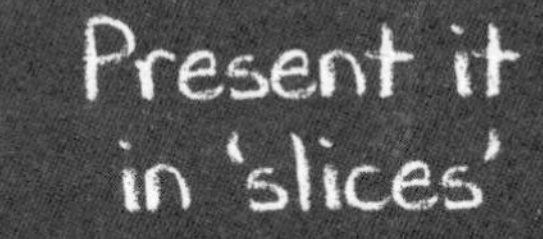

Present it in 'slices'

The resistance to my idea

How to carry through every idea

Meetings are known to reveal a person's character. Generally speaking, there are four personality types in meetings:

1. **The silent type** says nothing, is thereby usually proven right, and always thinks he or she knows better.
2. **The opportunist** is enthusiastic about every suggestion, especially those made or favoured by the boss.
3. **The 'master of the obvious'** announces the obvious with great conviction, as if he or she had just thought it up.
4. **The nay-sayer**'s purpose in life seems to be to pull apart other people's suggestions.

So how can you get a suggestion past these hell-hounds? A particularly effective method seems to be the Salami Tactic. Do not put your suggestion forward all in one go, but serve it in small, easily digestible slices instead. This portioning method has two advantages: first, the fear of a huge task or bold idea is reduced; second, a measured presentation allows the other participants to explore the idea themselves and think it through further. And, above all, this tactic does not allow the other participants to recognize your overarching intention. This makes it harder to fight against it. If there are ideological rifts, it is better to take small, isolated steps and concentrate on the matter at hand, not on the intended outcome.

And what do you do if someone tries to salami you? Simply ask: 'Is that everything?' Keep on asking until everything is on the table. Only then start negotiating, setting one slice of salami off against a slice of your own.

The origin of the term is unclear. Some sources say that in Hungary *Szalámitaktika* was the name given to the gradual takeover of power by the Communist Party.

Disassemble a truck into many small parts and a child can carry it.

5 Theory of R

How to make a go

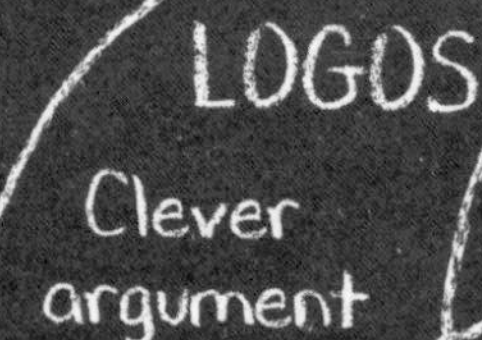

hetoric

od speech

Aristotle

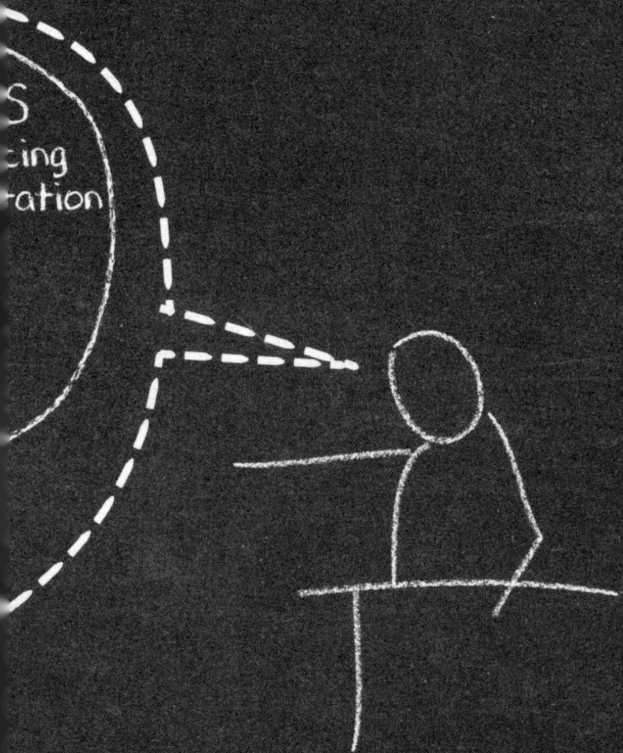

S

cing

tation

How to make a good speech

In his definitive work *Rhetoric*, Aristotle wrote that a good speaker has to have three things under control: the argument (*logos*), the presentation (*ethos*) and the audience (*pathos*). This may sound pompous, but it is just as valid today as in ancient times.

In Aristotle's day, there were only three different types of rhetoric: the first was judicial rhetoric, which dealt primarily with past events. Then there was epideictic rhetoric, which typically celebrated a person in the present (a typical example is a eulogy, which, Aristotle wrote, addresses the mourners rather than the dead). And, finally, there was deliberative rhetoric, such as political oratory, in which the speaker attempted to persuade the audience to carry out a certain action in the near future.

Aristotle, and later the Romans Cicero and Quintilian, established a complex five-point plan for writing brilliant speeches, which essentially boils down to this: you should put all the aces that you want to play up your sleeve in advance. Good preparation, in other words, is everything.

Aristotle considered rhetoric not as a tool to convince the audience, but as an art form to help present a persuasive argument. This was the end to which the speaker should employ rhetoric. Because people with good ideas are often poor speakers, he provided them with a toolbox full of rhetorical resources. So Aristotle was in fact the first person to prepare academics for their TED talks and keynotes. Below are six rhetorical tools:

1. **Anaphora**: repetition of a word or phrase, typical in political speeches: 'I demand justice. I demand understanding. I demand . . .'
2. **Inversion**: reversing the usual word order, such as in 'Infinite is his sorrow' (instead of 'His sorrow is infinite').
3. **Irony**: saying one thing when you really mean the opposite, e.g. 'I really enjoyed being stuck in that traffic jam.'
4. **Rhetorical questions**: questions that make a statement, e.g. 'Would you like shiny, glossy hair?'
5. **Analogies** (comparisons): 'He stood there like a dying duck in a thunderstorm' (banal) or 'He was as confused as a comma at the end of a sentence' (creative).
6. **Antithesis**: a contrasting thought to produce tension, e.g. 'He was beautiful, strong and . . . unhappy.'

In practice, the same applies to presentations as to speeches: read through your text aloud several times (one full sheet of A4 is about four minutes of presentation). Remember to integrate pauses. Look at your audience. Breathe deeply.

A good speech is one that induces the listeners to change their minds, while giving them the feeling that this change of opinion is their own decision.

6 Storytelling

How to make the lecture exciting

Today's lecture:
Algebraic equations
$a_n x^n + a_{n-1} x^{n-1} + \ldots$
$\ldots + a_1 x + a_0 = 0$

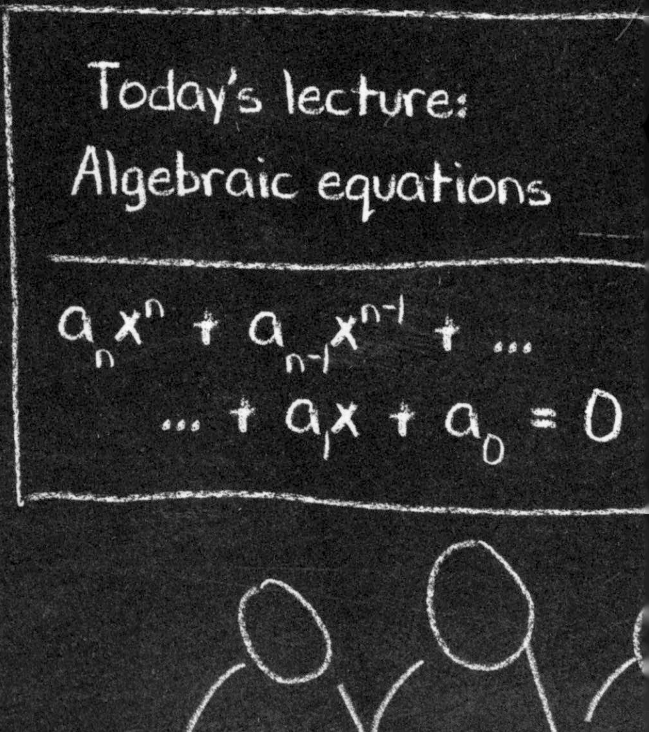

nost boring

William Labov·Walter Fisher

How to make the most boring lecture exciting

Why do all fairy tales begin with the phrase 'Once upon a time . . .'?

The answer is relevant for anyone who gives presentations: according to the sociolinguist William Labov, if we weave hard facts into narrative patterns, associations with well-known fairy tales are evoked in our memories which remind us of the pleasure of listening to them. With the consequence that our attention span increases. Classic fairy tales follow a particular sequence:

- **Abstract**: how does it begin? ('Once upon a time . . .')
- **Orientation**: who/where/when? ('A king and queen had a daughter . . .')
- **Complicating action**: the problem to be solved ('But all around the castle, a hedge of thorns started to grow . . .')
- **Resolution**: solution ('Then he stooped and kissed Sleeping Beauty. And she opened her eyes for the first time in many, many years . . .')
- **Evaluation**: what results from it? ('And they lived happily ever after.')
- **Coda**: what remains ('And the moral of the story . . .')

A lecture should be structured along the same lines. The idea is not new. Aristotle (see 'Theory of Rhetoric', p. 18) was already aware of the importance of emotion in speech-making. And in 1984 the communication researcher Walter Fisher came up with a radical thesis: people do not want logical arguments; they want good stories. Our life is not an Excel spreadsheet – it is a story with ups and downs. Fisher's idea is summed up in his famous 'narrative paradigm', which represents a break with classical rhetoric: we do not evaluate a story on the basis of arguments, but on the basis of how much we trust or believe in the story (can I identify with the subject or the people?) and its coherence (does the story make sense?).

Chris Anderson, the inventor of TED, says something similar about the three rules for a perfect TED talk: 1. Don't talk about a concept, a deficiency or a product; talk about an idea. 2. Focus on just one idea. 3. Talk about the idea in such a way that people will want to tell others about it.

The next time you have to say something in front of other people, start your talk with this sentence: 'Let me tell you a short story . . .' or 'On the way here, something strange happened to me . . .'

7 Principled N
How to reach an
Thing, no
Similarities, no
Good enough,

egotiation

reement

Roger Fisher·William L. Ury

person

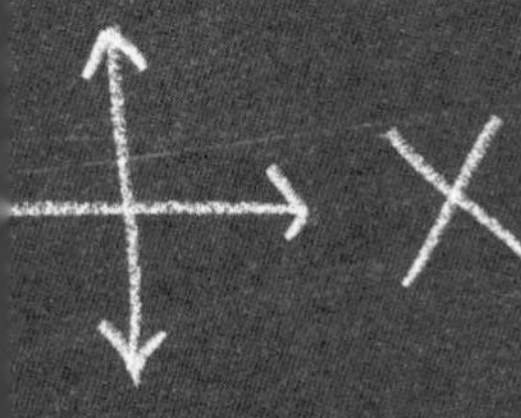

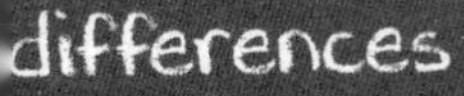

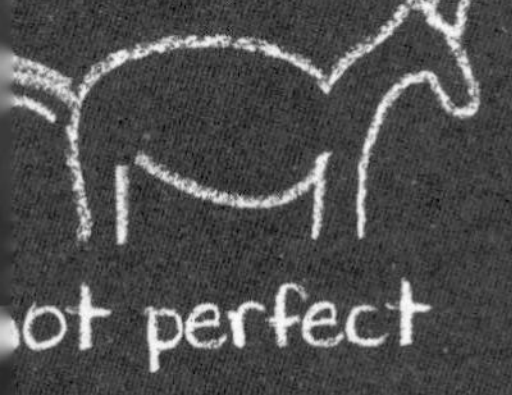

ot perfect

How to reach an agreement

Negotiation is the fine art of finding a solution to an apparently impossible situation. One of the best-known negotiating methods, 'principled negotiation', is based on the book *Getting to Yes* by Roger Fisher and William L. Ury.

Let's break down their strategy and apply it to real life: think about a complex situation – negotiating your salary with your boss, pocket money with your children, a ransom demanded by a blackmailer – and try to apply the following principles to the situation:

- **Thing, not person**: do not be distracted by whether you like the other person or not.
- **Similarities, not differences**: don't think: *I am in the weaker* [or stronger] *negotiating position.* Ask yourself: *What does the other person need from me? Do we have common interests?*
- **Good enough, not perfect**: you should not be aiming for the maximum possible. Because perfection is like the unicorn: it's rumoured to exist, but nobody has ever seen it. So, alongside your desired outcome to the negotiation, have a Plan B prepared before negotiations even start. This is called the BATNA Principle (Best Alternative to a Negotiated Agreement*)*. It offers the best alternative when an agreement can't be reached.

There are two schools of thought when it comes to negotiation: the first believes that you have to negotiate 'hard' and 'conquer' the other side ('It's not enough to win, someone has to lose'); the other recommends negotiating 'softly' in order not to put a strain on the relationship. 'Principled negotiation' falls into the second camp and recommends cooperative negotiation. Negotiating properly means that everyone gets more than they originally hoped for.

'You must never try to make all the money that's in a deal. Let the other fellow make some money too, because if you have a reputation for always making all the money, you won't have many deals.'

J. Paul Getty

8 The Feedba

How to criticize

Const

NO, BECAUSE...

NO!

Destr

k Method

D. L. Cooperrider·D. Whitney

tive

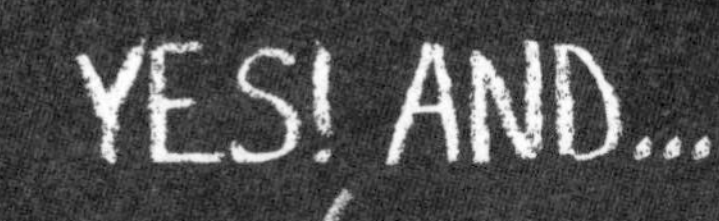

YES, BUT...

ive

How to criticize

Feedback is one of the most sensitive processes in communication. It is easy to hurt people with criticism, but false compliments are also unhelpful. Harsh criticism damages our self-esteem and can lead us to make unwise choices, but flowery compliments often make us too complacent.

As for the person giving the feedback: most people are prone to being critical, as it gives them a feeling of superiority. They feel like they need to crush bad or weird ideas.

Feedback can be analysed along two axes: it can be negative or positive and constructive or destructive. So this gives us four different types of feedback.

1. **'No' – negative, destructive feedback**: you are simply told the idea is bad without being given an explanation or offered an alternative. While this can be at times an effective feedback it seldom changes the behaviour of the receiver.
2. **'No, because . . .' – negative, constructive feedback**: you are told you're wrong and then you are presented with the correct answer. This is how old-school teaching works.
3. **'Yeah, but . . .' – positive, destructive feedback**: most managers have sooner or later heard about the importance of giving positive feedback. So they start off by saying something positive about your idea, just to deconstruct it afterwards and offer a contrary opinion ('The idea is good, but . . .').

4. **'Yes, and . . .' – the appreciative response**: try to find the one thing in the proposal that works and build on that. This goes back to 'appreciative inquiry', a method attributed to an American, David Cooperrider, that involves concentrating on the strengths, positive attributes and potential of a company or a person, rather than weaknesses. According to this theory, focusing too strongly on the flaws of an idea or project stifles the open and positive approach that is essential for good working practices.

Careful: of course, we sometimes have to deliver crystal-clear or even harsh feedback. But the point is, people learn better if they are offered constructive feedback. We know this from brainstorming sessions where the flow and fun increase the more positive the exchange. Collaboration, it seems, dies when the response is negative and ideas are killed before they are explored.

Whenever you are about to give feedback, ask yourself: 'How can I make this idea better?' rather than 'Why is this idea bad?'

9 Groupthink

What happens wh
same opinion

n everyone has the

Irving Janis

What happens when everyone has the same opinion

For a long time it was common knowledge that group decision making was better than individual decision making. Even today we often celebrate collaborations, consensual decisions and teamwork.

However, as early as 1972 a Yale psychologist, Irving Janis, pointed out in a spectacular, radical paper that sometimes also groups make very bad decisions. Janis had studied such debacles as Pearl Harbor or the Vietnam War. And what he found was that these groups had rejected critical opinions and outside information.

In the warmth of a like-minded group people reassure themselves that they are right, that their analysis is superior to that of outsiders, that their consensus is a sign of the strength of the group, when in fact they have been looking only for evidence that confirmed their objectives. And any doubts in the room were silenced because if everyone seems enthusiastic and agrees with the plan, we will feel reluctant to speak up – even if we have serious doubts. This, by the way, seems to be one of the governing principles of Donald Trump's leadership strategy: surround yourself with yes-sayers.

Janis called the phenomenon that occurs when the desire for group consensus is stronger than the urge to express an unpopular opinion 'Groupthink'. If this happens, the group is at risk of making very poor decisions. And even more: if many people are too sure of the same thing, they become radical and imprudent. Researchers have observed this phenomenon among jury members:

the greater the consensus, the harsher the judgement, and the surer the jury is that its verdict is correct.

When does groupthink occur?
Typically, when there is:

- High group cohesiveness
- High pressure to make a good decision
- Strong, persuasive, directive leadership

How can we avoid groupthink?
Janis suggested several steps for preventing groupthink. Here are two great recommendations if you are the leader of a team:

1. 'Give a high priority to airing objections and doubts.' In other words: encourage all group members to speak their mind. Even and especially if the opinion is unpopular.
2. Divide your team into two and form competing teams to study the same problem. Compare results.

'When all think alike, no one is thinking.'
Walter Lippmann

ethod

with you

Robert Greene

How many
words
you need

When the force is with you

Most theories in this book argue that good communication has to do with cooperation. But in reality it's sometimes a different story. It is no coincidence that the book *The 48 Laws of Power*, a compilation of classic power strategies by the American author Robert Greene, was a bestseller. Borrowing from this book, here are some negotiating strategies that won't make you popular, but might help you come out on top. (*Warning*: even if you prefer to convince people with good arguments rather than by mean tactics, you should know these tricks because they are bound to be used against you.)

Never argue hesitantly

If you are unsure about something, try not to show it to others. Doubt and hesitation will only dilute your arguments. With 'for and against' formulations, your adversary will see an opportunity to pounce. So only speak up when you're sure you want to follow through your argument, and stand your ground – even if your plan is flawed. We forgive bold people their mistakes, but have no confidence in doubters.

Talk less

Counterintuitively, you should not try to convince the other person by talking a lot. The more you talk, the more interchangeable and ordinary your arguments seem. Every triumph that you achieve through words is in reality a pyrrhic victory, because nobody likes to be argued into a corner.

11 Intercultur
Communic
How to negotiate

Linear-active

Multi-active

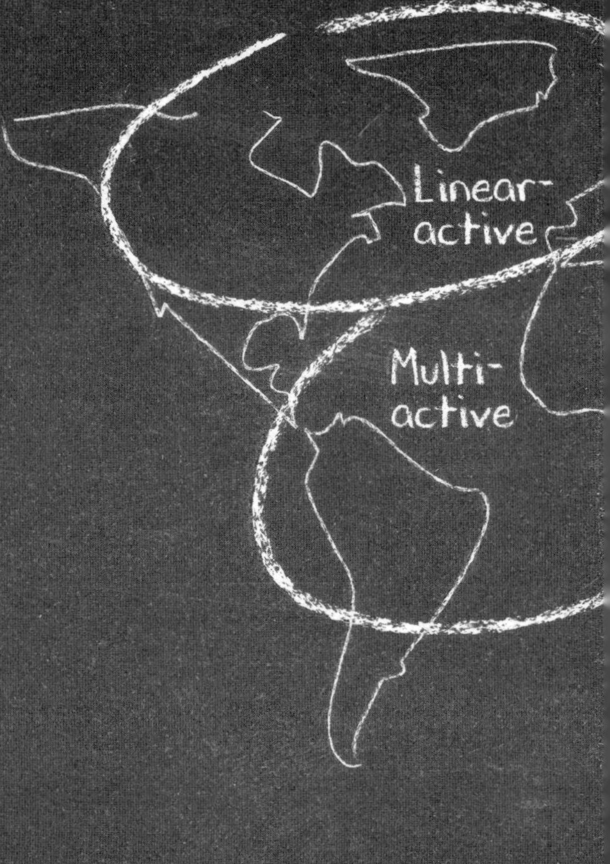

Act ignorant

We tend to be dazzled by intelligence and charisma. Try the opposite: make your adversary feel clever. He or she will be flattered and become inattentive. When your opponent's guard drops, you can attack. Acting stupid is one of the oldest stratagems around. As they say in China: 'Masquerade as a pig to kill the tiger.'

Give up

If you can't convince somebody, reassess your own situation: what will it cost me if I give up now? A smiling confession of your own defeat comes across as more self-assured than sullenness. And, what's more, the less interest you show, the less satisfied your adversary will feel.

'Oysters open completely when the moon is full; and when the crab sees one it throws a piece of stone or seaweed into it and the oyster cannot close again, so that it serves the crab for meat. Such is the fate of him who opens his mouth too much and thereby puts himself at the mercy of the listener.'

Leonardo da Vinci

10 **The Power**

When the force is

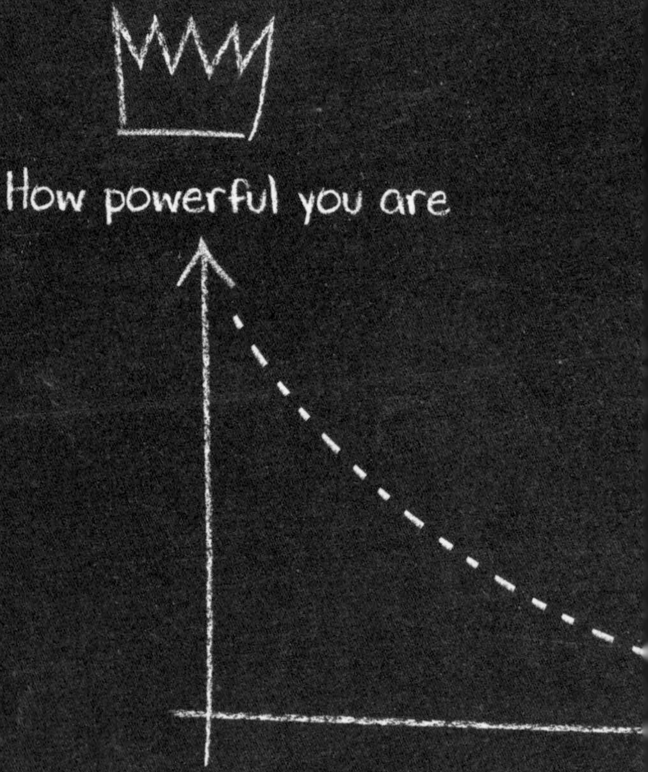

How powerful you are

Interculturethod
Communicowith you

How to negotiat

Robert Greene

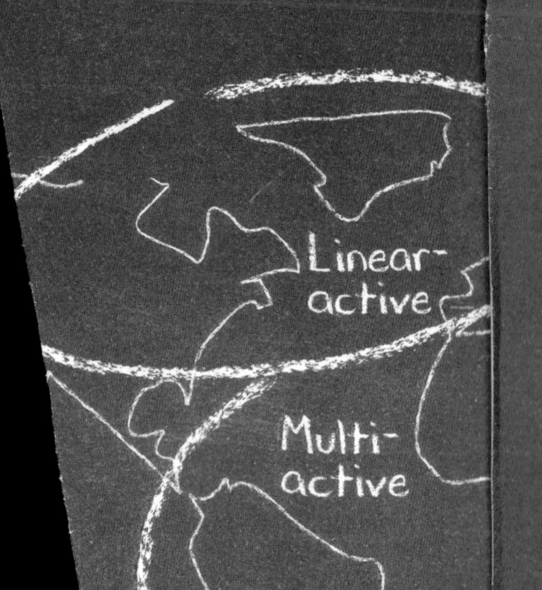

When the force is with you

Most theories in this book argue that good communication has to do with cooperation. But in reality it's sometimes a different story. It is no coincidence that the book *The 48 Laws of Power*, a compilation of classic power strategies by the American author Robert Greene, was a bestseller. Borrowing from this book, here are some negotiating strategies that won't make you popular, but might help you come out on top. (*Warning*: even if you prefer to convince people with good arguments rather than by mean tactics, you should know these tricks because they are bound to be used against you.)

Never argue hesitantly
If you are unsure about something, try not to show it to others. Doubt and hesitation will only dilute your arguments. With 'for and against' formulations, your adversary will see an opportunity to pounce. So only speak up when you're sure you want to follow through your argument, and stand your ground – even if your plan is flawed. We forgive bold people their mistakes, but have no confidence in doubters.

Talk less
Counterintuitively, you should not try to convince the other person by talking a lot. The more you talk, the more interchangeable and ordinary your arguments seem. Every triumph that you achieve through words is in reality a pyrrhic victory, because nobody likes to be argued into a corner.

Act ignorant
We tend to be
Try the opposi
or she will be
your oppon
stupid is on
say in Chi

Give up
If you
situat
smili
as
m
y

ion

broad

Geert Hofstede · Richard D. Lewis

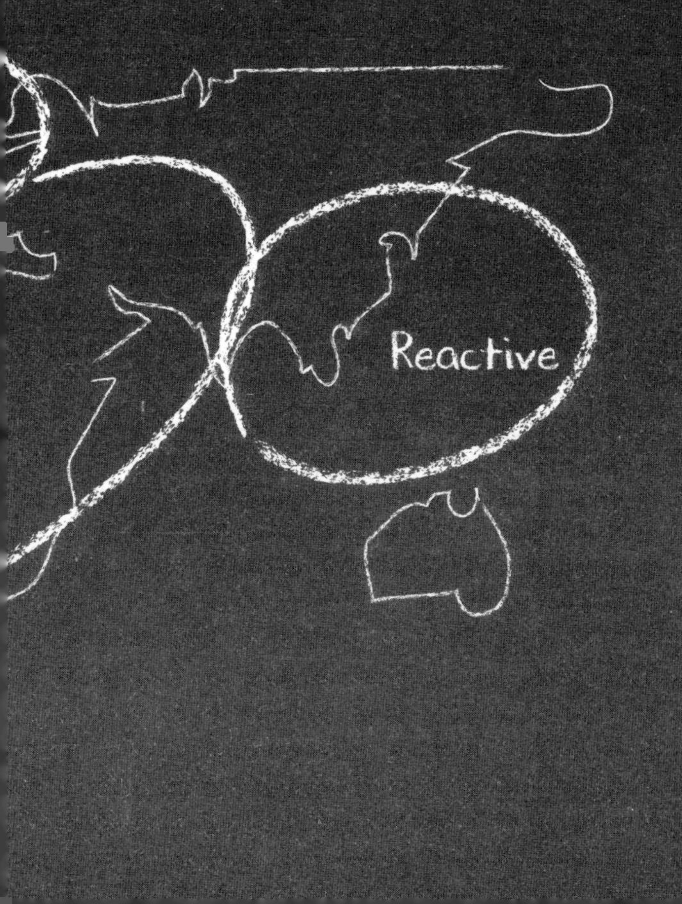

How to negotiate abroad

'There was once a Finn who loved his wife so much that he almost told her.' It's a joke, and yet not a joke. Because many Finns are indeed introverted, taciturn people.

Anyone who has come into contact with other cultures knows that stereotypes and prejudices can't always be trusted (the Scots are frugal, the Swiss are punctual, the Finns are introverted), but that they do often contain a germ of truth. Or, to put it another way, you might say that while many clichés are true, the more you get to know a culture, the more black and white turns to grey.

In order to get to grips with a culture it is not enough to master the language, as cultural idiosyncrasies are more apparent in the *way* we communicate than in *what* we communicate. What is required is so-called 'intercultural communication'. The term was coined by the Dutch social psychologist Geert Hofstede, while its most famous proponent is the British linguist Richard D. Lewis. In his classic book *When Cultures Collide* (2005), he defines three main cultural types: the linear-active, the multi-active and the reactive:

1. **The linear-active**, who include most of Western Europe and the USA, talk about as much as they listen, have fairly restrained body language, are polite but direct, like to deal in facts, and place value on the written word. They don't do two things at once.

2. **The multi-active**, such as Mediterraneans or Saudi Arabians, are loquacious, gesticulate a lot, are emotional, juggle with facts, place value on the spoken word, and do many things at the same time.
3. **The reactive**, such as the Japanese, Chinese and Koreans, speak less and try to get their counterpart to speak first; they have very subtle body language, are courteous and indirect, are non-confrontational, and place value on face-to-face communication.

But, contrary to what our schematic categorization might suggest, there are no pure alignments, only spectrums. Indians, for example, are hybrid – they are both reactive and multi-active. Canada is on the borderline between linear-active and reactive.

Linear-active: if you are intrigued by the questions 'What? When? How many?'

Multi-active: if you are intrigued by 'how' people communicate and relate to each other.

Reactive: if you're convinced by 'who' says it and their experience and authority.

SELF AND KNOWLEDGE

12 Self-Talk

How to (de)motiv

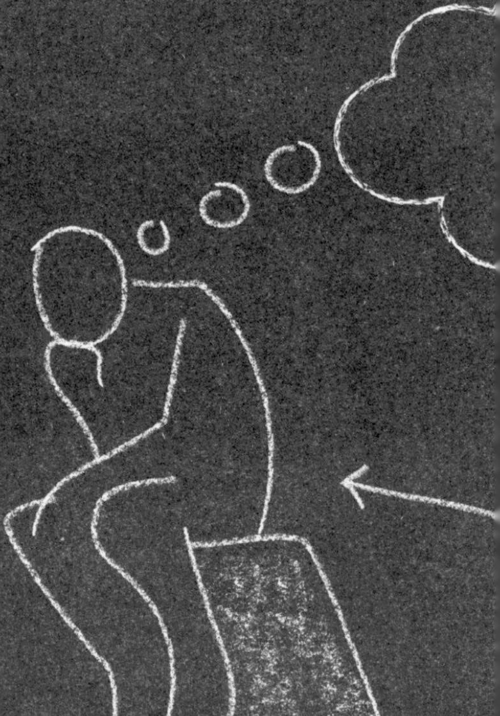

e ourselves

on't believe
verything you
hink

uguste Rodin, *The Thinker*

How to (de)motivate ourselves

There are two kinds of self-talk: the first is the unself-conscious babbling of little children as they play or the thinking aloud of contestants in TV shows such as *Who Wants to be a Millionaire?* These types of inner monologue were called 'egocentric speech' by the developmental psychologist Jean Piaget. He believed they were a sign of cognitive immaturity. Today, we know that thinking aloud is an excellent method for ordering our thoughts and improving concentration.

The second type of self-talk is the inner dialogue. We comment on our own behaviour in a similar way to a sports commentator reporting on events during a football match (the only difference being that the footballers can't hear the comments, whereas we constantly have our 'internal moderator' in our ear). In the field of psychology, this is considered to be a healthy form of self-evaluation. However, a distinction is made between positive and negative self-talk:

Negative self-talk typically contains one of these thoughts:

- **Generalization**: 'I have already been left twice – people will always leave me.'
- **Rash conclusions**: 'Why doesn't she call? I think she doesn't like me.'
- **Self-blame**: 'I should have done differently' or 'I'm a bad father.'

Positive self-talk is about breaking through the above negative patterns of thought. It's not about convincing yourself that life is great, but rather about freeing yourself from a cycle of negative thinking. For example, if you say: 'I'll never manage it', ask yourself instead: 'What can I do in order to manage it?'

In a nutshell: self-talk serves two different functions: first, concentration; and, second, motivation.

'[Talking to myself] is the only way I can be sure of intelligent conversation.'

'Edmund Blackadder'

13 Active Liste

How we are (not

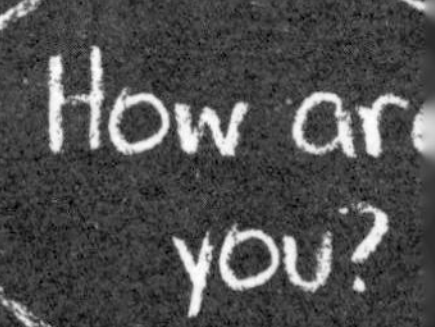

ing

ways) all ears

Carl Rogers·Richard Farson

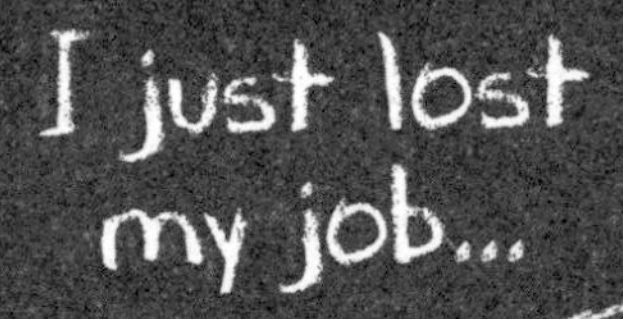

How we are (not always) all ears

Paradoxically, in our age of constant communication, the raw material of conversation has actually disappeared: listening. Genuine, real listening is a rare commodity and a great gift, because you are giving to the person you are listening to your most valuable asset: your attention.

Here are a few suggestions of how to do it right, based on the communication technique 'active listening' devised by Carl Rogers and Richard Farson in 1957.

Listen, don't talk

As the cartoon on p. 53 suggests, resist talking about yourself. Or as the radio host Celeste Headlee put it brilliantly in a TEDx speech: 'If they're talking about having lost a family member, don't start talking about the time you lost a family member. If they're talking about the trouble they're having at work, don't tell them about how much you hate your job. It's not the same. It's never the same. All experiences are individual. And, more importantly, it's not about you.'

Don't finish the other person's . . .

Some people have a tendency of impatiently finishing the sentence or thought of the person they are talking to. Although very slow thinking and talking can be irritating, don't interrupt, even if you think it might show empathy.

Your body language says a lot

Look the other person in the eye – but don't stare. Nod – but only if you want to agree with what they are saying or show that you have understood something important.

Notice the little things

Listen out for details in what they are saying and pick up on these later. This makes it easier to ask questions ('You mentioned that you spent a lot of time as a child at your grandmother's – what kind of relationship did you have with her?'). And it lets the other person know that you were really listening.

Be a friend, not a judge

Resist the impulse of giving the other person advice – unless of course they specifically ask for it. Instead, take the conversation back to an exciting, important part of the story: 'Earlier, you said that . . .' Take the person away from the smooth surface to deeper levels: 'How was it for you, when you . . . ?' Or encourage the person to keep talking by simply asking: 'And what happened next?'

'The most romantic gift: to listen to another's anxieties for one hour, without judgement or "solutions", as an analyst might.'

Alain de Botton

14 Small Talk

How to start a c
with strangers

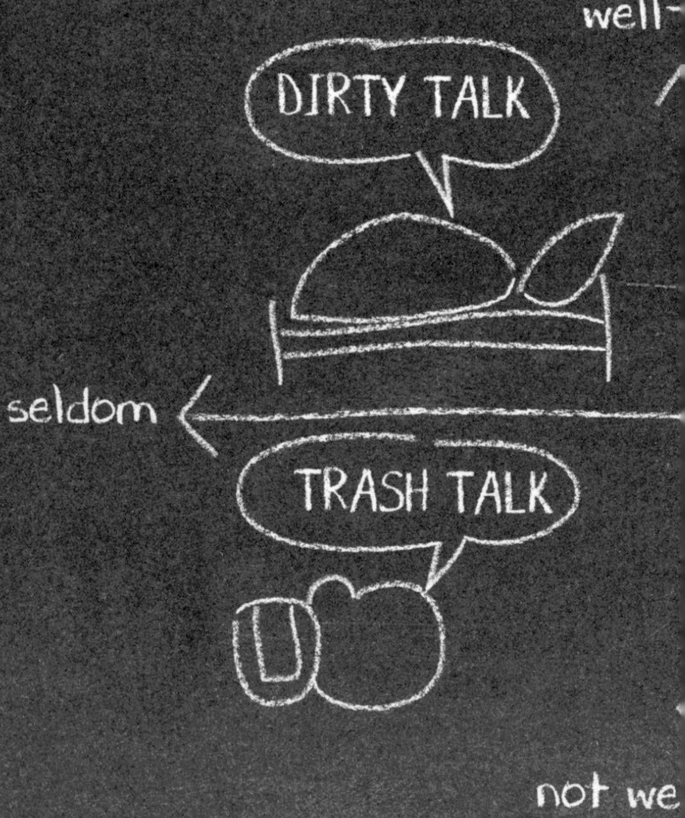

well-

DIRTY TALK

seldom

TRASH TALK

not we

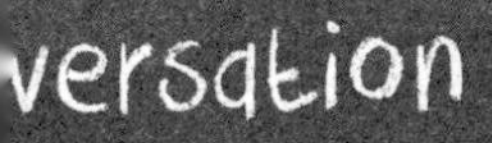

eant

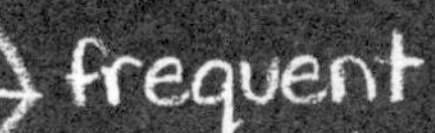

GOSSIP

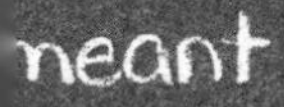

How to start a conversation with strangers

Small talk is actually something very big. Those who manage to start a conversation with strangers, break the ice and treat them like friends have the world at their feet (see 'proust's Questionnaire', p. 94). But it's incredibly difficult. There has been little serious research into the art of small talk and there are few reliable theories, but, nonetheless, here are some practical tips.

Ask for advice

People love giving advice. So, start your small talk with a request for advice: 'I want to buy a smartphone [or a cocktail or a book], but I can't decide which one.' Most people will happily open up. Then thank them for the tip and the other person will feel like a fireman who has successfully extinguished a fire. The psychology behind this: if you ask for advice, you create intimacy: intimacy makes rejection difficult. Therefore, if you want to influence someone, it is a good idea to ask that person for advice first.

Ask a second question

We often ask something and then wait for the other person to ask something back. This is not a conversation. Instead, use the old reporter trick and ask a second question. If you just asked 'Where did you grow up?', then a good follow-up question might be: 'How has that place shaped you?'

Don't ask: 'What do you do for a living?'

There are two kinds of people: those who like to talk about their job and go on and on about it; and those who are ashamed of their job, hate it or don't have one. The latter are reluctant to talk about this topic. The author Gretchen Rubin suggests this simple but powerful tweak to the usual 'What do you do for a living?' job question: 'What's keeping you busy these days?' Now the other person can choose what to talk about.

Don't start a conversation about things that interest *you*

Most people like to talk about themselves. This leads to us not listening any more, but simply waiting for our turn to speak. But a conversation is not a PowerPoint presentation. Don't pitch your topics. Rather be the one person in the group who is interested in the other person's topics. As Bill Nye put it: 'Everyone you'll ever meet knows something that you don't.'

Listen

The way people deal with you depends on how you present yourself: arrogant, worldly-wise or dull posturing brings out the same behaviour in your counterpart. The supreme rule when making small talk comes from the radio host Celeste Headlee: 'Enter every conversation assuming that you have something to learn.' People forget what they talked about with you, but not how they felt in your presence.

> 'We have two ears and only one mouth so that we can listen twice as much as we speak.'
>
> *Epictetus*

15 The Iceberg

What happens be

So, how was
school today?

Model

u the surface

Sigmund Freud

OK...

What happens below the surface

One of the most frequently cited and simplest but also most inscrutable of all communication theories is the Iceberg Theory.

Sigmund Freud, the founder of psychoanalysis, believed that human behaviour is governed above all by the unconscious – like an iceberg, where only the tip protrudes from the water, while the usually much bigger and mostly invisible part is below the surface. (At this point, it should be mentioned that we do not know for sure who came up with this brilliant metaphor – it certainly wasn't Freud; some say it was Hemingway, who in the 1930s claimed that an author does not have to explicitly reveal the deeper meaning of a story (see 'The Six-Word Rule', p. 84). It is sufficient if, like an iceberg, only a tenth is visible above water.

If we apply this rule to communication, we could say that the visible, conscious part of a discussion is the factual level (*what* we say or *what* we talk about), while the unconscious part is the interpersonal level (*how* we say it and what we really *mean*) – see 'Lasswell's Communication Model' (p. 148) and 'Watzlawick's Axiom Theory' (p. 90). This means we can control the factual level, we can select our words consciously, but our gestures, facial expression and tone of voice will betray our unconscious secret hopes, repressed conflicts, traumatic experiences, base motives and animal instincts, and appeal to the other person's unconscious. The interpersonal level decides how we will be perceived and how we perceive others.

The more we know about another person's values, patterns of behaviour, motives – in other words, the more we see of the iceberg – the better we can understand the person's words and actions. The best way to 'lower the waterline' of your opponent or partner is to show more of yourself. If you, for example, want someone to admit something, start by talking honestly about your own mistakes.

'Fear and hope are alike underneath.'

Richard Ford

16 The Spiral o

Why we don't da

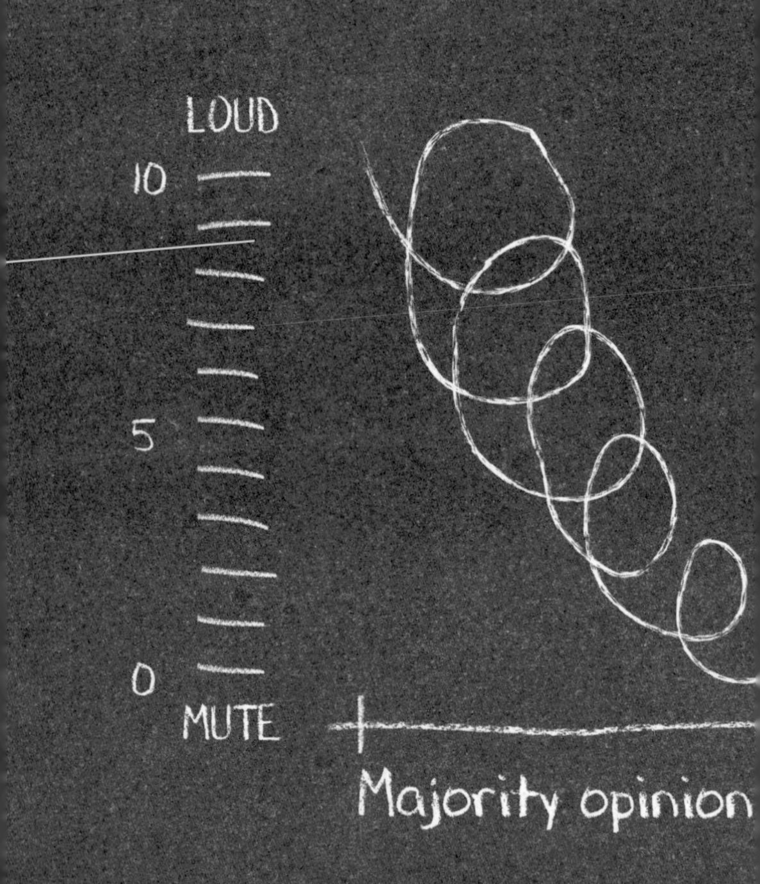

Silence

state our opinion

Elisabeth Noelle-Neumann

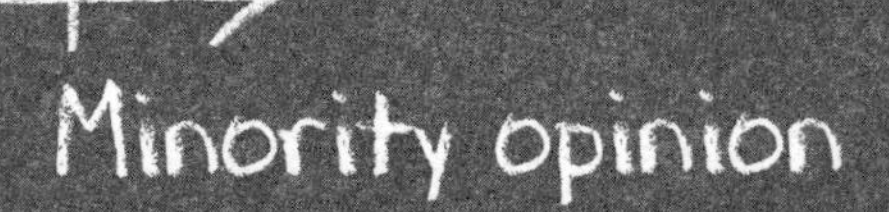

Why we don't dare state our opinion

Let us assume that you have a five-hour train ride ahead of you, and in your crowded compartment a person starts talking about tightening the asylum laws. Would you like to talk to this person or not?

This is the 'railway test', which the German social scientist Elisabeth Noelle-Neumann used to examine who sticks up for their opinion in public and who doesn't. Her hypothesis: the willingness of people to voice their opinion in public dwindles in situations where they believe that the majority opinion is different from their own. In other words, we do not like to be of a different opinion to others. If we notice that the group majority has a different opinion to ours, we remain silent. This phenomenon is called the 'spiral of silence' and can be explained by these six points, of which the last two are arguably the most important:

1. Most people have a fear of isolation and observe the behaviour of others to assess which opinions will be accepted or rejected. 'We fear isolation more than being wrong,' wrote Alexis de Tocqueville in the nineteenth century.
2. We exert pressure on each other: we pull a face, roll our eyes or turn away when someone says something that does not comply with the prevailing opinion.

3. Fear of isolation and a pressure to conform occur unconsciously. We do not think about the extent to which we are guided by public opinion.
4. We tend to conceal our opinion if we think that it will expose us to group pressure. If we feel public support, however, we tend to express our opinion loudly and clearly.
5. If consensus on a subject prevails in a group, it is unlikely that a spiral of silence will begin.
6. The number of people who share an opinion is not necessarily significant. A minority opinion can appear to be a majority opinion if its proponents appear confident enough and represent their opinion in public forcefully.

We become quieter if we believe that we are in the minority.

17 The Speech

How words can t

PLEASE LOOK TO
THE RIGHT

Act Theory

er actions

J. L. Austin

Like this.

How words can trigger actions

You can do an incredible amount with words. *How to Do Things with Words* is also the name of the well-known book by the British philosopher J. L. Austin from 1962, in which he substantiated 'language theory'.

He argued that in day-to-day life we distinguish between 'doing' and 'talking' but that there is in fact no difference. Speaking is also an action. His thesis: sentences have a 'propositional' meaning (this is the information contained in the sentence), which can be 'true' or 'false'. But sentences also have an 'illocutionary' meaning. This means that we are doing something when we speak, including something essential ('doing something *in* saying something'). Examples include requests, warnings, threats, recommendations. Such an illocution can succeed or fail – for example, if you don't take the speaker seriously, the act of speaking has failed. Then there is a third dimension, the perlocution. Here it is about the extent to which whatever was said has consequences – so whether the person being addressed acts on what is said or has a change of mind because of it ('doing something *by* saying something').

Let's take an example. If you say to a couple who happen to be sitting next to you: 'I hereby declare you husband and wife', then the 'proposition' is the same as what a vicar would say at a marriage ceremony in a church. The difference: the sentence is just words. But spoken by a vicar the sentence has weight and effect; it is 'illocutionary' and seals the marriage. And with a bit of luck it is also perlocutionary, if the married couple stick to their vows in future. The sentence of the vicar thereby triggers subsequent actions.

The Speech Act Theory explained in two sentences: 'What do we do when we speak? What impact do we have when we speak?'

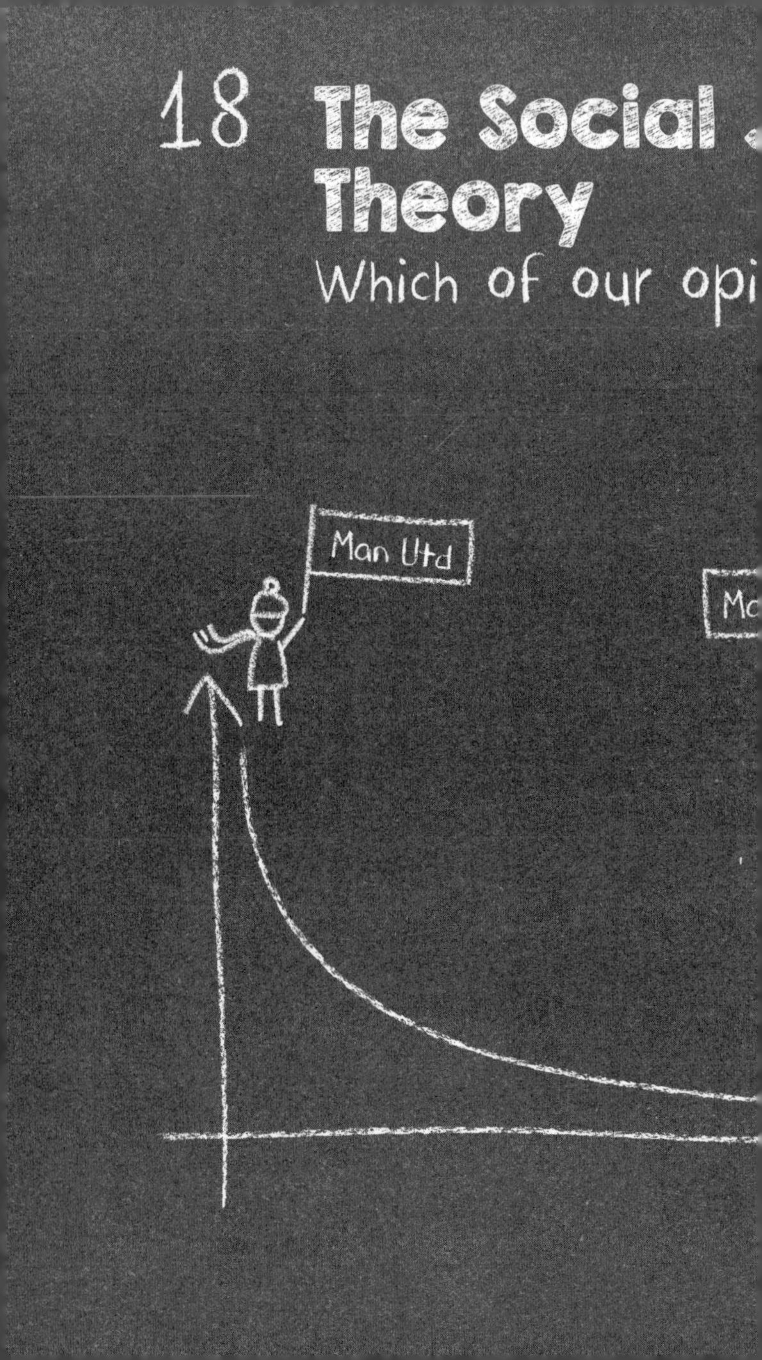
18 The Social
Theory
Which of our
Man Utd

ns never change

Muzafer Sherif · Carl Hovland

(impossible position)

Which of our opinions never change

A question that continues to preoccupy researchers into communication is this: when do people allow themselves to be persuaded about something and when not? Why is it that some of our attitudes are deeply ingrained and not up for discussion (e.g. allegiance to a particular football club), while we change others at the drop of a hat (favourite TV series, for example)?

An explanation is offered by the Social Judgement Theory. According to this theory, there are three factors that play a role in persuading us to change our opinion:

1. **The anchor point**: this is our basic preferred attitude. This attitude is hard to budge, and we are unlikely to change it, regardless of what information we are given. So, for example, if we were to discover that the players of our favourite football team were manipulating games, we might be shocked, but it wouldn't put an end to our long love affair.
2. **Room for manoeuvre**: here it is about which alternative attitudes we find acceptable, regardless of our own. These are attitudes that we can accept without having to hoist our anchor. This approach can lead to a change of opinion in the long term.

3. **Ego involvement**: the most complicated part: what does our ego have to say? Take the death penalty, for example, which clearly contradicts the anchor point 'human rights', leaving little room for manoeuvre. But it is conceivable that if we were personally affected by a murder, we might feel vengeful towards the perpetrator and change our mind, at least briefly.

The stronger our anchor, i.e. our firm position on an issue, the harder it is to be persuaded by a different opinion. The stronger you pull at another person's anchor, the stronger their resistance. (How can you can succeed anyway? See 'Six Principles of Persuasion', p. 6.)

If you can't change your mind, then you're not using it.

19 **The Sorry M**

How to apologize
other person for

Roy J. L

FORGIVE

(+) resentful

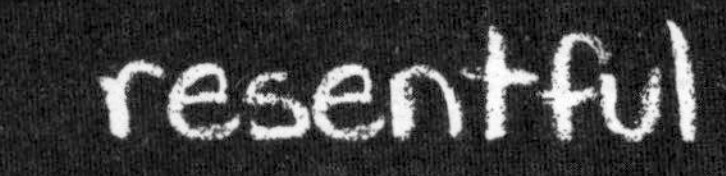

(−) mean

(−)

atrix

roperly so that the
es and forgets

cki·Beth Polin·Robert B. Lount Jr

dysfunctional

FORGET

⊕

How to apologize properly so that the other person forgives and forgets

Apologizing is one of the most difficult interpersonal communication situations. A few years ago, a team of researchers from Ohio State University tackled this issue and played through a variety of approaches. We translate their findings into strategies:

Use 'I' sentences

Apologizing means taking on full responsibility for something. Sentences like 'I'm sorry that your feelings were hurt', or 'I'm sorry that you're so angry', should be avoided (because what you're implying is: it doesn't have anything to do with me that your feelings are hurt). Say it like it is: 'I'm sorry that I hurt your feelings.' According to the research, a person is most likely to forgive and forget if you admit full responsibility for what you did.

Don't justify your actions

It is a natural reflex to try to justify your own actions. But also an idiotic one. Because a justification is in effect a denial of the apology. The following sentences are particularly counterproductive: 'Come on, it wasn't that bad!' or 'I can't help it.' The injured person will be more inclined to forgive if you come up with a reason rather than a justification: try to explain your action without being defensive. Most effective of all are an explanation and an admission of guilt combined.

Avoid 'but' sentences

An apology in which the word 'but' crops up is almost never understood as an apology but as an excuse. Avoid at all costs.

Don't ask for forgiveness

Asking for forgiveness is rarely effective. According to the research, you can spare yourself the bother. Nobody likes to grant absolution.

Change yourself

Even the most honest apology is worthless if you repeat the same mistake three times. Making an apology is above all a commitment to making a change and an offer to make amends.

When it comes to apologies, keep in mind there are only two ways: you can apologize begrudgingly or sincerely. Choose the latter.

20 **White Lies**

How to answer th

'How do I look?'

TRUTH

'You look fat.'

question:

Sanjiv Erat · Uri Gneezy

'You look great.'

'You've lost weight.'

How to answer the question: 'How do I look?'

The truth is, all people lie. In certain situations – such as when we are under pressure, have to justify ourselves, or want to make a good impression – we tend more towards fibbing and telling tales than when we feel relaxed and self-secure. But, from an ethical point of view, not every lie is bad. You might, for example, lie in order to protect someone. In communication theory, lies fall into two categories: do I benefit from the lie or does the person I lied to benefit? This results in four different outcomes.

1. **White lie – only the person lied to benefits**: this is a fine, selfless lie in which you risk potential loss to help someone out. Here, you typically put yourself in the position of the person and, for example, defend the existence of Santa Claus in the knowledge that the lie will be exposed in due time. This altruistic lie gives us a good feeling.
2. **Grey lie – both the liar and the person lied to benefit**: 'You've lost weight!' Grey lies are often part of cultural norms. In many situations, when you ask: 'How are you?', you expect a lie in response: 'Thank you, things are great!'

3. **Black lie – only the liar benefits**: although you are guilty, you reject all accusations: 'No, I didn't take the money!' It is often also a bold promise, a proactive lie: 'If I am elected I will never raise taxes . . .' Here, bare-faced lying is used to your own advantage.
4. **Red lie – no one benefits**: this is the lowest form of lying. Saying something with complete awareness that the other person knows the statement to be false, even if you sometimes end up also inflicting damage on yourself: 'The largest audience ever to witness an inauguration.'

'If you tell the truth, you don't have to remember anything.'

Mark Twain

21 The Six-Wor

How to sum up a

Rule

hole life in six words

Ernest Hemingway·Larry Smith

A novel by
Ernest Hemingway

For sale:

baby shoes,

never worn.

How to sum up a whole life in six words

No one knows whether the story's true, but it is a good one anyway. Ernest Hemingway was sitting having a drink with some writer friends at Lüchow's restaurant in New York. They were talking about this and that, and eventually moved on to what the ideal length of a good novel might be. Hemingway claimed that he could write a novel in six words: the others each bet ten dollars that he couldn't. Whereupon Hemingway wrote: 'For sale: baby shoes, never worn' on a napkin. Six words, behind which lies a tragedy. Those who don't gulp when they read this must have hearts of stone.

In 2006, Larry Smith, founder and editor of SMITH magazine, asked: 'Can you tell your life story in six words?'

A dumped 27-year-old guy wrote: 'I still make coffee for two.' 'Cursed with cancer. Blessed with friends' came from a nine-year-old cancer survivor. The singer Moby confessed: 'Dad died, mom crazy, me, too.' And George Saunders summed life up beautifully: 'Started small, grew, peaked, shrunk, vanished.'

Smith's formal restriction proved not to be limiting but stimulating, and in the spirit of the pithy language used in social media, the logic of the 140-character tweet and the compulsive succinctness of texts, six-word memoirs became a hit.

The thinking behind the abbreviated form: language is beautiful, and its diversity and complexity are a reflection of the depth of human sensibility. But it is also an excellent tool with which to beat around the bush. The Six-Word Rule is not a rejection of sprawling, convoluted sentences or endless digressions; even Hemingway was of the opinion that not every idea can be pared down. But before writing (or speaking), you should ask yourself these questions: What do I really want to say and can I say it more succinctly?

If it's important, keep it short.

LOVE AND FRIENDSHIP

22 Watzlawick
How relationships

Axiom Theory
annoyed
is grumbling
is annoyed.

How relationships fail

An axiom is a valid truth that needs no proof. At the end of the 1960s, the communication theorist Paul Watzlawick, together with other researchers, came up with five axioms to explain how interpersonal communication – especially in relationships – fails.

1. You cannot not communicate

A man comes home, sits down, stares into space and is silent. His wife looks at him and asks him how he is. He says nothing – and yet he communicates something. It is immediately clear that something must have happened. Even if you say nothing, you are saying something.

2. All communication has a relationship aspect and a content aspect

The content aspect is what we say. The relationship aspect includes *how* we say things, but also *who* says something (see 'Schulz von Thun's Communication Model', p. 110). *Who* says something and *how* it is said always weigh heavier than *what* is said. If we are offended by a complete stranger, it affects us less than if our partner offends us. Also keep in mind Albert Mehrabian's *7%–38%–55% Rule*. If we are talking to someone about our feelings, this is the impact our words, tone of voice and body language have: our words are 7 per cent, our tone of voice 38 per cent and our body language 55 per cent responsible for whether that person likes us.

3. Communication is always about cause and effect
A woman is annoyed because her partner is grumbling. The man is grumbling because the woman is annoyed. In other words: we seldom quarrel with ourselves – it will always take two to tango.

4. Human communication makes use of analogue and digital modalities
In Watzlawick's terms, 'digital' means verbally and 'analogue' means non-verbally – in other words, eye-rolling, a smug smile, ambiguous intonation. If the two levels do not correlate, then we're not on the same page.

5. Communication is symmetric or complementary
Relationships between partners are either symmetrical (equal) or complementary (unequal). Symmetric means that we talk at eye level (in the relationship); complementary means that there is a kind of hierarchy (for example, between teacher and pupil). If we do not agree whether the communication is complementary or symmetrical, it becomes problematic.

Everyone hears what you say. Friends listen to what you say. Best friends listen to what you don't say.

23 Proust's Que

How to ask good

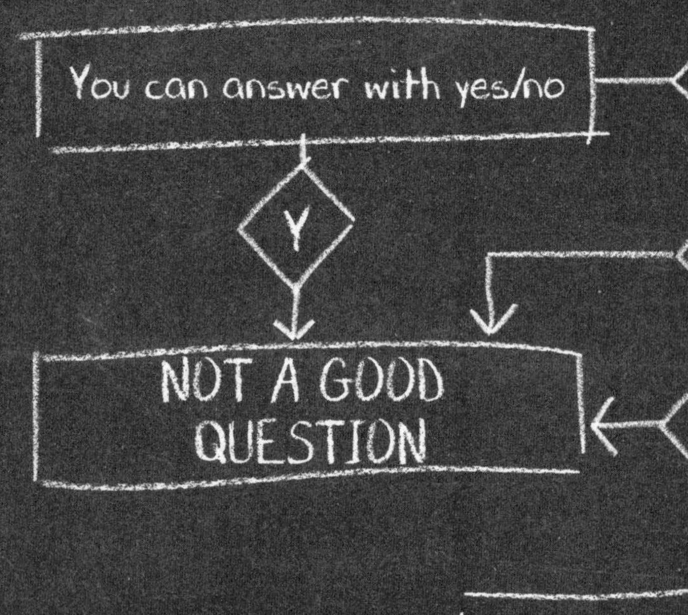

stionnaire

uestions

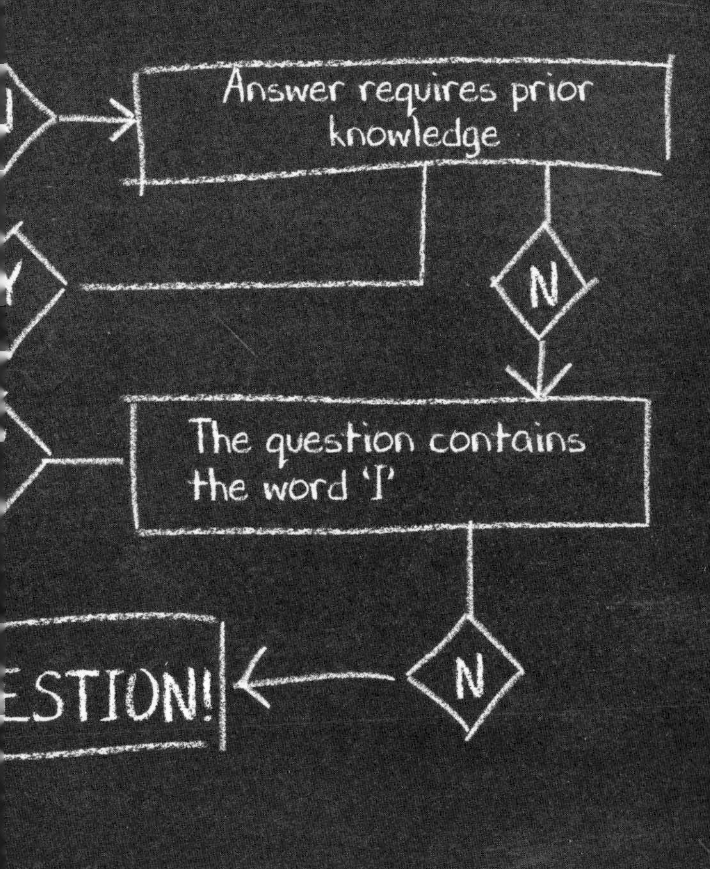

How to ask good questions

In the late nineteenth century, light conversation (or 'small talk' in modern English – see 'Small Talk', p. 56) was crucial to the success of an evening. Being refined was not about saying the right thing without having to think too hard, nor was it about getting the other person to laugh at one's charming, witty remarks. Instead, the ideal neighbour at a dinner party was the one who had mastered the fine art of asking questions. The explanation for this is simple, and truthful, and can be summed up with this rule: we do not appreciate those who are brilliant, but those who make us feel brilliant.

But because it is extremely difficult to ask the right question in the right situation, a small crib sheet soon circulated around European salons. It consisted of questions that seemed innocent but which bared the soul, such as 'Who would you prefer to be?', 'How would you like to die?' and 'Which characteristics do you most appreciate in a man?' The author of the questionnaire remains unknown to this day. In 1885, Marcel Proust (then only thirteen years old) answered the questionnaire at his friend Antoinette Faure's birthday party. In 1924, Faure's son published Proust's answers; since then it has been known as 'Proust's Questionnaire'. The fact that he didn't invent it, but simply filled it in, speaks in favour of the charm of the above rule.

Proust's questions have three key qualities:

1. They are open questions that you cannot answer with yes or no.
2. The questions require no prior knowledge; in other words, there are no right or wrong answers, only honest ones.
3. They are questions that centre on your counterpart rather than on you.

We all admire people who give good answers. But we admire those who ask good questions even more. The people we remember most are the ones who really listen.

24 Nonviolent

Why we find it d

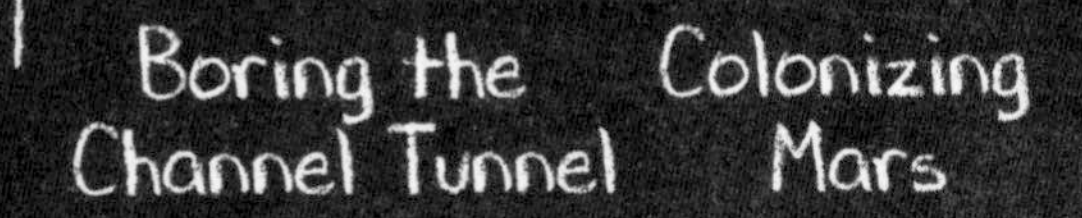

ommunication

icult to be friendly

Marshall B. Rosenberg

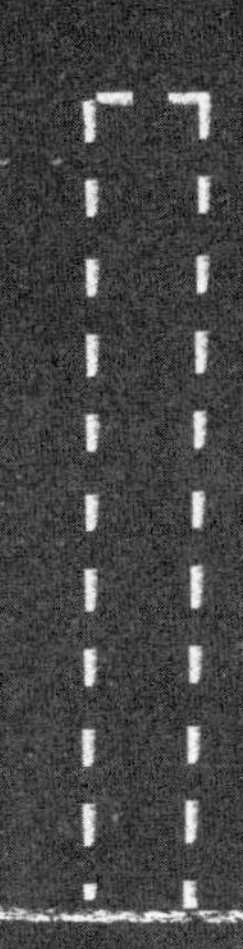

ompleting
unway 3 at
Heathrow

Nonviolent
communication

Why we find it difficult to be friendly

Psychologists generally agree that conflicts need to be dealt with, but the question is: how? The American psychologist Marshall B. Rosenberg (1934–2015) developed the idea of nonviolent communication based on the premise that it's not what you say, but how you say it. He distinguishes between speaking snappishly, 'language of the jackal', and speaking from the heart, 'language of the giraffe' (giraffes have the biggest heart of any land animal). This may sound like mumbo jumbo, but it comes closer to reality than most management jargon. The language of the jackal causes the speaker to feel superior and the person being addressed to feel bad. Typical examples of jackal language:

- **Analysis**: 'That's wrong, because . . .'
- **Criticism**: 'The mistake you made was that you . . .'
- **Interpretations**: 'You do that because . . .'
- **Appraisals**: 'You're smart/lazy, you're right/wrong . . .'
- **Threats**: 'If you don't do it immediately, I'll have to . . .'

According to Rosenberg, statements like these are 'desires in disguise'. Because we have not learned to ask for something politely or to express our wishes constructively, we resort to aggressive language. And aggression leads to counter-aggression or submissive subjugation.

Giraffe language, on the other hand, works like this:

- Observe without evaluating: 'You always look out of the window when I want to talk to you.'
- Acknowledge and define your own or others' feelings: 'I'm worried.'
- Acknowledge needs and take them seriously: 'I want to know how you're doing.'
- Express clear and achievable objectives based on these needs: 'Please tell me what you need, so that we can talk about it.'

But why is it so difficult to be friendly? Often, we ourselves are the problem. Take the so-called 'attribution error': if we arrive late, there was a lot of traffic. If others arrive late, they set off too late (or for people with a negative frame of mind, the other way round). We are by nature prone to pass judgement, and what's more, it is easier to blame someone else than to think about *why* something happened.

The essence of normal communication: we all like to be right. The essence of nonviolent communication: we are better off if we resolve a dispute than if we win it. Or in the words of Marshall Rosenberg: 'Would you rather be right . . . or happy . . . ?'

25 The Cooper

How we should e

to be understood

A German walks
into a bar.

Dry

tive Principle

ress ourselves in order

Paul Grice

ne Martini,
please.

Nein, I said
one!

How we should express ourselves in order to be understood

People's three biggest fears: loving someone without being loved in return; searching for friends and not finding any; saying something and not being understood. There is no solution to the first two. For the third there is at least a principle. The British philosopher Paul Grice (1913–88) dedicated his life to this problem and in 1975 finally formulated the so-called Cooperative Principle, a basic rule for effective communication:

'Make your conversational contribution such as is required, at the stage at which it occurs, by the accepted purpose or direction of the talk exchange in which you are engaged.'

You might be thinking that Grice could have done with some language training himself, but let's take a closer look at what the Cooperative Principle is actually all about. According to Grice, speaker and listener want to (and have to) behave cooperatively. This means that one person wants to be understood, the other to understand. In order for this to work, Grice proposed four conversational maxims:

1. **Maxim of quantity**: say enough for your counterpart to understand, but don't say too much, or you will cause confusion.
2. **Maxim of quality**: tell the truth, don't speculate, don't dupe the person into believing something different.

3. **Maxim of relevance**: don't say anything irrelevant, don't change the subject.
4. **Maxim of manner**: avoid ambiguity, vagueness, verbosity and volatility, and stick to a logical argument.

If we follow these maxims, then, as a general rule, we will be understood. But what happens if we don't follow them, which is the case in most of our conversations?

- We can violate the maxims without being noticed. That's called 'lying'. ('Did you wreck the car?' 'No, I didn't' – although you did.)
- We can violate the maxims deliberately by saying something else but expecting the listener to understand the message correctly. That's called 'flouting'. (A typical form is irony: you look out of the window to see the storm intensify. You then turn to your friend and say: 'What wonderful weather!')
- We can refrain from cooperation. That's called 'opting out'. (If you say: 'My lips are sealed', this implies you know something, but won't talk about it and this will end all communication.)

Only say what is true and important, and express it clearly and simply.

26 **The Expect
Violations T**

How much distanc
people

Int

ncy
eory
we keep from other
Judee Burgoon

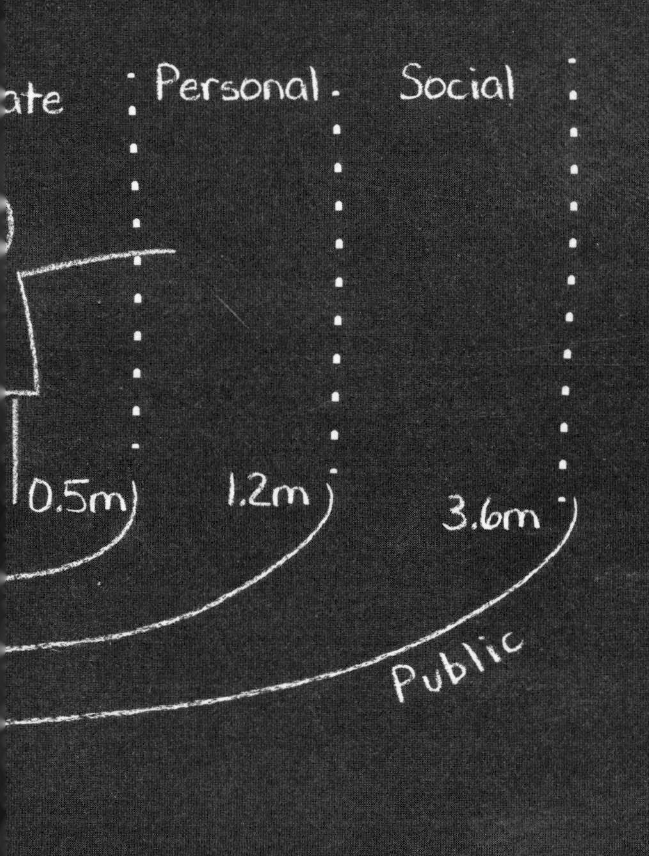
ate
Personal
Social
0.5m
1.2m
3.6m
Public

How much distance we keep from other people

Perhaps you know the feeling: you're sitting in the cinema, the film hasn't started yet, the auditorium is barely a third full, and several rows are completely empty. Someone comes in, looks around, walks past the empty seats – and sits down right next to you! The feeling that you now have is called 'expectancy violation'. You expected something different – that the person would find an empty seat, not one right next to you. In 1985, the American Judee Burgoon developed the Expectancy Violations Theory, which analyses how our expectations of another person affect the way we respond to unanticipated violations of these expectations or social norms. According to Burgoon, the following rules apply in the Western world with regard to keeping our distance:

1. **Intimate space (elbow room)**: up to 50 cm. Within this space, we expect to be touched by the other person. It is reserved for close family, lovers and pets.
2. **Personal space**: 50–120 cm. The typical distance we keep from somebody we are talking to.
3. **Social space**: 120–360 cm. The distance we keep from people we do not know, with whom we do not communicate, but whom we have nothing against.
4. **Public space**: 360 cm or more. This distance is best explained if we ask ourselves: which people do we avoid?

Of course, it is not only about distance, but also about physical and eye contact. If someone turns away from us while we are speaking, it violates our expectations of the conversation. This is most easily observed in romantic relationships, where the usage of smart-phones and social media is for many a strong sign of divided attention and a source for trouble.

The distance we keep is also influenced by cultural and situational norms. Different distance rules apply to dancing in a club and studying in a library. In Switzerland, people greet one another with three little kisses; in the USA, this would be regarded as too close for comfort.

When in Rome, do as the Romans do.

27 Schulz von Communica

Why we should t
about how we ta

Hey, it's green!

Impaired

aun's
on Model

to each other

.o each other

Am I
driving or
you?!

mmunication

Why we should talk to each other about how we talk to each other

It's an archetypal misunderstanding: A couple are sitting in a car and the traffic lights turn green without the driver noticing. The passenger says: 'It's green.' The driver replies testily: 'Am I driving or you?'

This example comes from Friedemann Schulz von Thun. His 'communication square' does not count as a theory in the narrower sense, but it breaks down the many pitfalls of communication in a clearer way than other approaches. According to Thun, every message has four layers:

1. **Content** (what I am informing myself about).
2. **Appeal** (what I want to achieve).
3. **Relationship** (my relationship to the receiver).
4. **Self-disclosure** (what I show of myself).

Our example contains the content layer ('The traffic light is green'), the appeal layer ('Come on, drive!'), an allusion to the relationship (the passenger wants to help the driver) and the self-disclosure layer (the passenger is probably in a hurry). These are the four facets of the sender's message.

The person receiving the message – in this case, the driver – does so with his own four 'ears'. On the content layer ('The traffic light is green') the two people are still in agreement, but the driver interprets the appeal ('Come on, drive!') differently (i.e. 'Why are you so slow?') and finds this insulting. He reacts accordingly: 'Am I driving or you?'

We encounter this kind of flawed communication all the time: 'Hey, what's this in the soup?' – 'If you don't like it, eat bread.' 'When will you be ready?' – 'Stop hassling me!'

The way we understand messages is determined by the sender's and receiver's previous history, the context, the tone and many other non-verbal signals. How can we solve misunderstandings? By talking to each other about how to talk to each other; in other words, by practising 'meta-communication'. Because good communication occurs when intention and understanding are in harmony.

'What is thought is not always said; what is said is not always heard; what is heard is not always understood; what is understood is not always agreed; what is agreed is not always done; what is done is not always done again.'

Konrad Lorenz

28 Game Theo

Why it's worth t

Jo

If she says
'yes' first,
then I'll
say 'yes' too...

...or
no?

ng to each other

on Neumann·Oskar Morgenstern

Why it's worth talking to each other

The twentieth century was the century of mass murder. Two world wars took place within a period of thirty years. In-between, there was some lousy diplomacy. The logic of this period was: 'The clever side never gives in and comes out on top.' To win you have to take action, not negotiate. Europe was in ruins by the time the game was over.

During this period, John von Neumann, a mathematician, and Oskar Morgenstern, an economist, developed their famous Game Theory. This theory examines conflicts in which the result for all participants depends on decisions made by others – as in negotiations. Game Theory is based on the observation that people in conflicts behave in the same way as they would when playing a board game: they want to win, but do so by sticking to the rules of the game, otherwise it won't work. How do you win but still follow the rules? The solution: by approaching and talking to each other. Or, in the words of game theorists, by cooperating.

Let's take a simple example. At some point, most adults decide not to give each other Christmas presents any more. The pressure to consume is annoying, and, in any case, what do you give a person who has everything? But typically some people still do buy a present, even if they agreed not to. The person who gets the gift but didn't give one in return now has a bad conscience; the person who gave but didn't receive is disappointed. The result: conflict.

There are only two logical solutions and both have to do with communication: you have to decide whether (a) everyone or (b) nobody gets a gift. But this super-simple Game Theory solution can only be achieved if both sides go along with the plan and if they make a binding agreement to stick to it: two complex actions that people find hard to carry out.

'Meeting jaw to jaw is better than war.'

Winston Churchill

29 Second-Or

How your therap

I see a
man who
can't see
the wood
for the
trees

Tre

r Observation

talks to you

Niklas Luhmann

s!

1st order

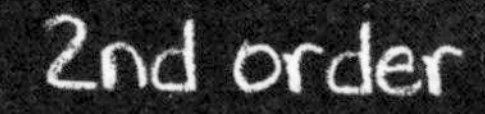

How your therapist talks to you

What does your therapist do when talking to you? He or she makes a so-called 'second-order observation'.

A first-order observer sees the world as it appears to him or her: the world is simply there. The second-order observer, however, ascribes *what* the first-order observer sees to *how* it is seen. *Important*: we cannot observe ourselves observing (which is also why therapists can't treat themselves). This is often referred to as the 'blind spot'. In other words, we are unaware of the way in which we observe; we cannot see that we cannot see. So by identifying someone's blind spot, the second-order observer might open up a new perspective, and make that person aware, for example, of the fact that he or she could just as easily see something differently.

An example: a couple want to move in together, but she has one of those flats that you simply wouldn't want to give up: a great location, low rent, a big balcony. And the flat would be big enough for two. He hesitates, because he feels that he would be intruding and that it would still feel like her flat. They cannot afford a new flat for the two of them. She sees only the potential advantages of her flat, he sees only the potential disadvantages. Both are first-order observers and are talking at cross-purposes.

A second-order observer could give them another perspective: the couple could move into the woman's flat, but on the condition that it becomes a shared flat that they move into as if it were new. This means she has to first 'move out' of her flat, before the two of them 'move in' and refurbish it.

Despite the fact that most people constantly think about themselves, it is impossible to observe yourself while doing (or thinking) something. We can only train ourselves to be more aware of moments when we act or think according to old (and bad) habits. But in order to recognize these patterns we need a second observer.

We can't see that we are seeing something.

30 Transactio

Which 'I' do you

Where's the toothpaste?

Probably i
bathroom

Analysis

to communicate?

Eric Berne

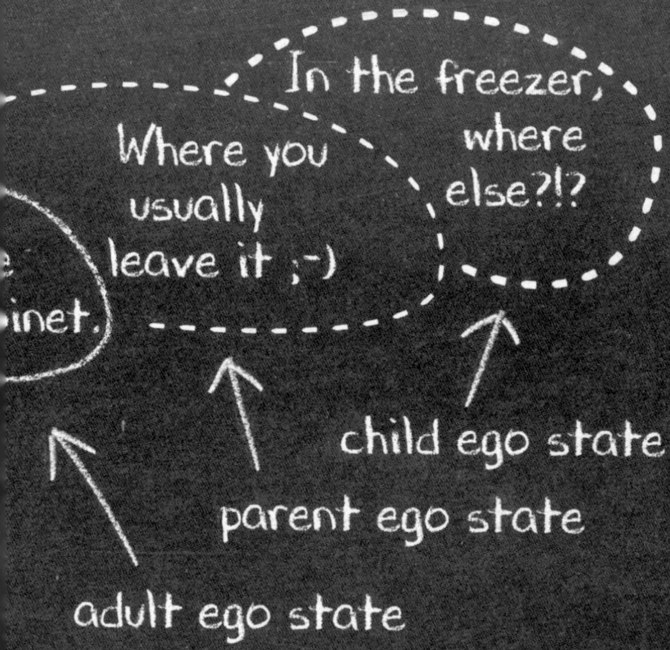

In the freezer, where else?!?

Where you usually leave it ;-)

child ego state

parent ego state

adult ego state

Which 'I' do you use to communicate?

Here are two of the greatest interpreters of human communication:

- **Sigmund Freud** (1856–1939), the founder of psychoanalysis, believed that hidden pleasures and fears from our childhood are the motivation behind our communication problems.
- The psychiatrist **Eric Berne** (1910–70), however, believed that you do not have to go on a painful journey into your past to get to know yourself; it is enough to observe yourself in communication with others.

In 1964, Berne proposed in his book *Games People Play* a counter-model to Freud's theory, a book which due to its simplicity and clarity became a bestseller in the genre of communication and self-help books. According to Berne, it all starts with the three 'ego states' we adopt in relation to others:

1. **The parent ego state**: we all are a little like our parents. This is evident when we patronize others or tell them what they should or should not do. But also when we act thoughtfully, empathically or helpfully.
2. **The adult ego state**: we act like adults when we communicate in a considered, controlled and relaxed way. In other words, when we treat the other party respectfully and respond to criticism factually and constructively.

3. **The child ego state**: we also carry in us the child that we once were. We are unrepentant, defiant, silly or anxious. But positive qualities such as imagination, curiosity and learning are also evident in our childlike communication.

All states occur in one person. So what use is transactional analysis in practice? When we communicate, it is always from one of these ego states. We are not always aware of this; but it is most evident when we observe ourselves. Let's suppose that a proposal we put forward in a discussion is rejected by the group. If we react in an offended way or respond defiantly, we are in child mode. If we weigh things up rationally and realize that our proposal was no good, we are in the adult mode. But if we argue morally that the others are wrong because we are right, we are in parent mode.

If communication does not work, you should ask yourself: what state am I in at the moment – parent ego, adult ego or child ego?

31 Parenting

How to talk to
have any of your

What parents teach

A

B

A = Child

B =

en (even if you don't
n)

What teachers teach

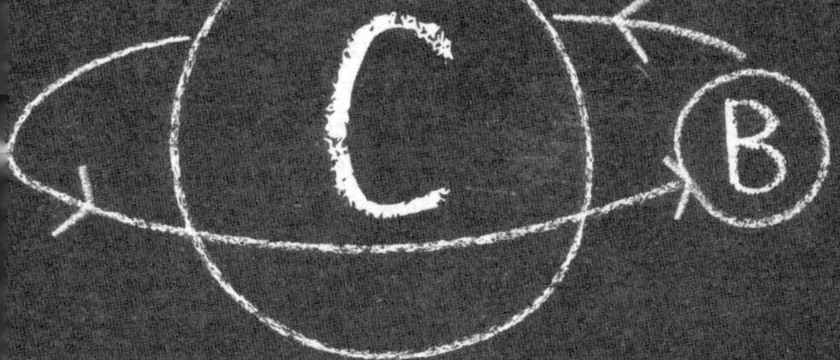

th · C = Sun

How to talk to children (even if you don't have any of your own)

If you've ever asked a child: 'How was school today?' or tried to explain to a toddler that it shouldn't feed washing powder to the cat, you know that good communication can be more complicated than algebra. So here are some tips from parenting experts:

- **Be a role model**: actions speak louder than words. A child won't understand that he shouldn't scream if you scream at him.
- **Correct content, not form**: the child says: 'I draw horsy.' That's fine, as long as she is drawing a horse.
- **Be consistent**: 'no' means 'no' – even when the child is having a tantrum at the supermarket check-out. *Loophole*: only make threats that you can go back on without losing face. So don't say: 'If you don't stop right away we won't go away on holiday.'
- **Implement threats immediately**: children learn more quickly and effectively if you carry out your threats straight away. Instead of taking away a toy once for a whole week (long duration, small effect), it is better to take away the toy ten times for two minutes (small duration, big effect).
- **Praise an action, not the child**: 'What you're doing is great' is better than 'You're great.'

- **Ignore bad behaviour**: when a child does not behave according to your expectations, but isn't putting himself or others in danger, it is better to ignore him than to rebuke him ('selective attention').
- **Offer alternatives**: give your child different options, but never more than two, and only if an alternative makes sense (there is no alternative to teeth brushing).
- **Tell a child what she should do, and not what she shouldn't do**: it's better to say: 'Please slow down' than 'Don't run!'
- **Ask questions that can be answered**: 'How was school today?' is as difficult for your child to answer as it would be for you to answer: 'How was March to April 2014 for you?'
- **Adults were children once, too**: these rules of communication apply to all ages.

'It is easier to build strong children than to repair broken men.'

Frederick Douglass

32 L'Esprit de l

When we think o

Knowing what
we want to say

he best arguments

William Lewis Hertslet

after the conversation

during the conversation

When we think of the best arguments

'The term *l'esprit de l'escalier* ("staircase wit") refers to opinions and ideas that we express with clear, polished pithiness – and which always occur to us too late. Afterwards, when we slowly descend the stairs, we are suddenly much smarter than before.' This is how William Lewis Hertslet described the term in his bestseller *Der Treppenwitz der Weltgeschichte* (*Staircase Wit of World History*), which was published in 1882.

Over 130 years later it is still as relevant as ever. We all know how it feels when our brain starts to work only when the pressure of a stressful situation subsides. Before a date or job interview, we know exactly how we want to present ourselves, but when the small talk starts, we can't think of anything clever to say. Then, once the conversation is over and we have closed the door behind us, we come up with razor-sharp arguments and witty lines. In psychology, this phenomenon when your nerves fail under pressure is called 'choking': you 'choke' on the expectations.

Many studies have dealt with this phenomenon, and have all come to the same conclusion: paralysis by analysis. If you start thinking, you lose. If you try to be quick-witted, you can't think of anything to say. When you go for that all-important penalty kick, your confidence plummets. Psychologists recommend four tricks:

1. Expose yourself repeatedly to the same situation (so-called 'practice under pressure'), whereby the situation loses its uniqueness.
2. Wait five seconds before answering – your answer might not be any cleverer, but it comes across as weightier.
3. Not so easy: imagine that you're not in an interview but sitting in the pub with friends.
4. Keep in mind that although being quick-witted can be impressive in an interview, it is seldom required in most jobs.

'Nothing in life is as important as you think it is while you are thinking about it.'

Daniel Kahneman

WORDS AND MEANINGS

33 The Framin

What kind of ima

Erving Gof

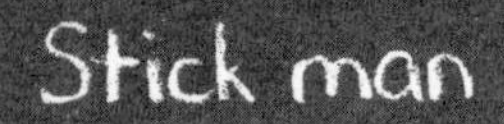

Child's d

Effect

we have of the world

·Daniel Kahneman·Amos Tversky

What kind of image we have of the world

In communication, there is a fundamental rule: *how* something is said and by *whom* – the 'narrative context', or frame – determines how something is understood. To take one example, if a sensational piece of news is printed in a reputable newspaper, we are more inclined to believe it than if it is reported in a tabloid.

This observation was made by Erving Goffman, who described this form of interpretation as 'framing'. If we look at a picture in a museum, we know that it is art even if it looks like a stick figure drawn by a child. This is because we have learned to recognize the frame 'modern art'. Another example: if we go to a restaurant, we know how to behave – how to interact with the waiter, how to handle a knife and fork, and what to do with the menu. We know this because we know the frame 'restaurant'. In his seminal work *The Presentation of Self in Everyday Life*, Goffman uses the imagery of theatre and acting to describe human social interaction. He believes that we each adapt our behaviour to each frame and are therefore a different person in each situation. This means that there is no such thing as authenticity. We are one person when we are at work, another when we talk to our parents and quite another when we are lost in a foreign city and have to communicate with strangers.

Daniel Kahneman and Amos Tversky famously showed how different ways of phrasing frame a dilemma and affect people's responses to a choice. This logic is used to great effect in advertising. For example, two yoghurts are on sale: one is '90% fat-free' and the other is touted as having a '10% fat content'. Although both contain equal quantities of fat, people tend to choose the yoghurt advertised as 'almost fat-free', because the frame for the yoghurt purports that it is a fat-free, healthier product. The bottom line is: we seldom make rational choices.

There are no objective or authentic messages. Everything that is being communicated is always framed. And if you want to decode a message, try to understand the frame.

34 McLuhan's

Why the medium

To what extent it c

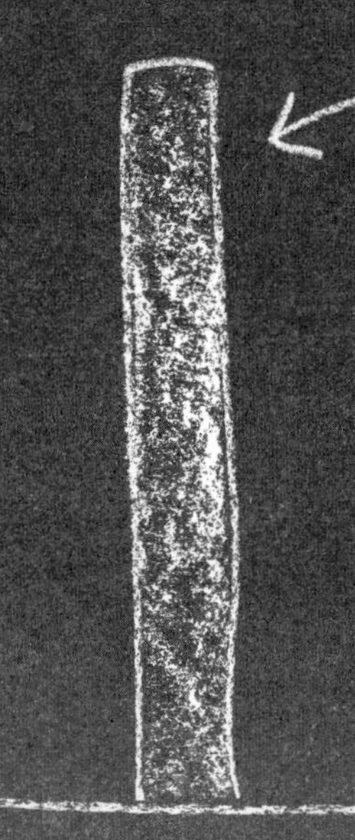

edia Theory

the message

Marshall McLuhan

nges your behaviour

none

#JeSuisCharlie
#occupywallstreet
#brexit

Why the medium is the message

The Canadian media scholar Marshall McLuhan (1911–80), who generally shunned the limelight, became the world's most talked-about intellectual in 1967. This was because he had summed up the media revolution – the transition from print to TV – in a single sentence: 'The medium is the message.' The sentence is not as simple as it first appears.

What does it mean?

It does not mean what you might initially think, i.e. that the medium has become more important than its message. (*A hint*: McLuhan's theories never focus on the obvious, clear-cut or logical.) Rather, the sentence means that the medium is not important because of its message, but because it can change our behaviour, our thinking and our lives.

And what does that mean?

If we use the word medium, we are usually only referring to the channel via which information is transmitted. McLuhan believed that this channel is more formative for our culture than the message it carries. If the message changes, we simply change our minds. But when the medium changes, we change our behaviour. This sounded crazy in the 1960s. But since the advent of social media, and since we have started to reflect on the ways in which mobile devices dominate our everyday lives, it makes much more sense. Suddenly, his meaning is crystal-clear: it's not *what* we read on our smartphone that changes our behaviour, but *that* we are reading it on our smartphone. (What makes our smartphone so fascinating that we stroke it more than our new-born child? – See 'The Uses and Gratifications Theory', p. 152.)

'We shape our tools and the tools shape us,' wrote McLuhan. He also wrote: 'People don't really read newspapers. They just climb into them every morning like into a hot bath.' Was there ever a better description for the Internet? In his time, McLuhan was taken more seriously by hippies than academics. This was a double misunderstanding, because, as a conservative Catholic, he was opposed to the media developments he described.

The news doesn't change us; the medium does: take a minute and make a list of five things that have changed in your behaviour since using a smartphone. Now ask yourself: what changes do you regret? And finally: what would it take to undo them?

35 The FoMO P

What happens if

smartphone

Things you've missed
while reading
this text

enomenon

u don't look at your

A. K. Przybylski et al.

...that are really important.

What happens if you don't look at your smartphone

The Internet has multiplied the number of ways in which we communicate. While we still communicate one to one (in a personal email, for example), we now also often communicate one to many (e.g. in a Facebook post or WhatsApp group message).

One of the most important elements of online communication is self-presentation: we only want to show our best side. We post photos of perfectly prepared dishes, perfect holidays, perfect parties, perfect scores. And this starts a vicious circle: whenever we feel bored or alone, we look at our smartphone. But what are we looking for? We basically want to see that others have seen us – a 'like', a 'share', a 'retweet' is proof of that. But when looking at social media we also see the apparently perfect lives of our friends – which we are not part of – and how these lives are being 'liked' and 'shared'. Scientists call the 'uneasy and sometimes all-consuming feeling that we're missing out – that our peers are doing or in possession of more or something better than we are ' – 'Fear of Missing Out', or FoMO. A team of psychologists at the University of Essex, led by Andy Przybylski, came up with this name.

People under the age of thirty-five suffer more from this phenomenon, men more than women, teenagers more than adults, unhappy more than happy people. To clarify: it's not a question of *really* missing out on something; it's about the *feeling* of having missed out on something. We've all been there: when we're feeling down, bored or stressed out, we check our smartphone. But all this does is make us feel even worse. Smartphones act like an accelerant when it comes to FoMO – and thereby corroborate the fifty-year-old 'McLuhan's Media Theory' (p. 140): 'The medium is the message.'

'In the twentieth century "I think, therefore I am" no longer applies, but rather "Others are thinking of me, therefore I am."'

Peter Sloterdijk

36
Lasswell's
Model
How to recognize
WHO
WHAT
says
to

mmunication

ke news

CHANNEL

a

hich

vith

EFFECT

vhat

?

How to recognize fake news

The term 'fake news' has become ubiquitous in recent years. But what is fake news? Basically it is an aggressive way to influence people. But, fake or not, all news is influencing – something which the inventor of public relations, Edward L. Bernays, took full advantage of. (*Fun fact*: Bernays was the nephew of Sigmund Freud, founder of psychoanalysis.) His most famous work, which he wrote in 1927, was originally entitled *Propaganda*, but he later changed the name to *Public Relations*. Bernays wrote: 'The conscious and intelligent manipulation of the organized habits and opinions of the masses is an important element in democratic society . . . We are governed, our minds moulded, our tastes formed, our ideas suggested, largely by men we have never heard of.' It's a pretty good description of the world we live in, isn't it? But how should we interpret Bernays's strangely euphoric-sounding text?

Like this: freedom of expression is a democratic right. When everyone expresses their opinion, millions of opinions and interests collide, and chaos ensues. So either you create order out of the chaos by implementing restrictions (which would be a dictatorship) or you have to make your own opinion as attractive as possible and market it as such. You can use all the tricks of the trade to come out on top. You can manipulate a little, cheat a little, exaggerate a little to make yourself more interesting. Ideas can be presented as attractive or less attractive, and it is up to individuals to decide whether they want to follow them. This means: PR and advertising or even fake news cannot force us to do anything we don't want.

If you want to analyse (fake) news, a good starting point is the light-hearted model developed by the American sociologist Harold D. Lasswell in 1948, which still works astonishingly well today: for example, to separate fakes from facts. The formula is: '*Who* says *what* in *which* channel to *whom* with *what* effect':

- **WHO?:** by answering 'who' said it, we divert our attention to the sender. Lasswell called this 'control analysis': who is talking? What is their aim? Who are their allies?
- **WHAT?:** by looking at 'what' is being said, we give attention to the actual message (the 'content analysis') – to identify the aim behind the message we can, for example, ask: how are women or people of colour represented? What does the phrasing imply?
- **WHICH?:** by answering the 'which channel' question we make a 'media-analysis': why are they using this channel? How can they afford it? Who paid for it?
- **TO WHOM?**: the 'audience analysis' can, for example, reveal something about the aim of the sender: why are they talking specifically to these people?
- **WITH WHAT EFFECT?:** with the 'effect analysis' we ask: how did the audience react? What does this tell us about the sender?

Lasswell was concerned with the effects of mass media. But his message also applies to interpersonal communication. His formula is a simple way to sharpen your senses for propaganda. Wherever it's coming from.

37 The Uses ar
Theory

What we want w

ESCAPE

FUN

Gratifications

n we're online

Elihu Katz

IDENTIFICATION

INFORMATION

FRIENDS

What we want when we're online

What makes screens so attractive was a question already being asked by researchers in the early days of television. In 1960, the sociologist Elihu Katz claimed to have the answer. His 'Uses and Gratifications Theory' was radically different from other media effect theories. He believed that media consumption was an active, voluntary decision, and consequently did not ask what media does to *us*, but what *we* do with media. He identified five reasons why we use media and what we use it for (spoiler alert: the first three reasons are obvious, the second two interesting):

1. **Information and education**: we consume media to discover what has happened but also to educate ourselves.
2. **Entertainment**: we consume media for our emotional or aesthetic pleasure.
3. **Identification**: we consume media because we identify with people we see on screen.
4. **Integration and social interaction**: we consume media so that later we can talk about what we saw or heard with others. Today the so-called 'second screen' comes into play: we watch TV and at the same time consume via a second screen like a smartphone, with the consequence that we are alone and yet not lonely (for example, #doctorwho or #strictly) – see 'The FoMO Phenomenon' (p. 144).

5. **Escapism**: we consume media to escape reality. Everyone is familiar with this behaviour: we immerse ourselves in a film, a game or the Internet and forget about ourselves.

It is important to notice that according to this theory media do not force us into anything – we decide for ourselves what we want to use.

'When I die I want my tombstone to say "Free WiFi" so people will visit more often.'

Unknown

38 The Encodi Model

How messages c differently

dominant-hegemonic

neg

/Decoding

e understood

Stuart Hall

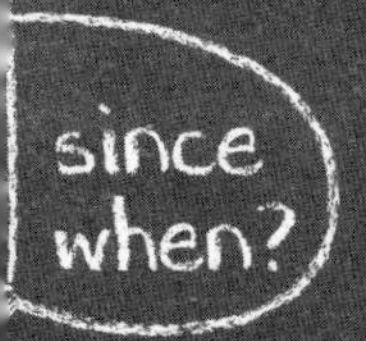
since when?

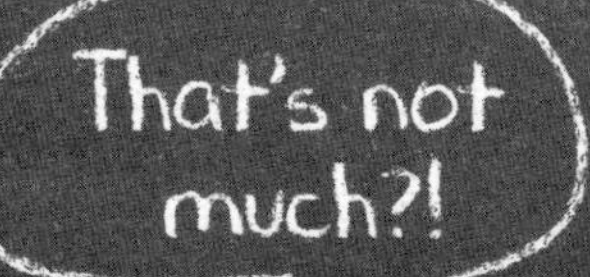
That's not much?!

ed

oppositional

How messages can be understood differently

A small but significant question: is what I can hear the same as what you are saying?

Every child that has ever played Chinese Whispers knows the answer: not always.

One of the greatest communication theorists, Stuart Hall (1932–2014), was of the same opinion. In fact, he took the idea further. He believed not only that we are capable of *mis*understanding, but that we play an active role in understanding, *per se*. We interpret, or 'decode', the same message differently, depending on our social class, our level of knowledge and our cultural background. But, above all, the way we understand a message also depends on how we *want* to understand it. An example is the cult 1960s TV series *Star Trek*. Many fans interpreted the series as a classic science fiction adventure in space. But the gay community saw the close-knit relationships between the men and the rainbow crew (black African, Asian, Russian, Vulcan) as an allusion to the fact that some of the characters were gay. It is irrelevant that *Star Trek*'s creator, Gene Roddenberry, denied this, because, according to Stuart Hall, the message can be changed once it has been received. In other words, *Star Trek* fans saw in the series what they wanted to see.

The Encoding/Decoding Model contradicts the classic sender–receiver model, according to which the recipient plays a passive role. Hall argued that the way we *receive* a message is an active and never clear-cut process, so that the message can always be understood differently. The sender encodes the message with a particular intention. The receiver decodes the message in order to understand it. And this decoding can happen in three different ways:

1. **Dominant-hegemonic**: the desired reading – we understand the message the way it was intended
2. **Oppositional**: we oppose or dismiss the intended meaning
3. **Negotiated**: a combination of the two

A message is more than just what is said. It changes depending on how it is understood.

Let's put this into practice: if you are a leader, always make your team repeat to you how they have understood your message. (That is, by the way, the reason why co-pilots always repeat what they just heard the pilot say.)

39 Visual Com

How we interpre

evil

unication

gns

funny

How we interpret signs

When we want to communicate something, we use signs – words, gestures, facial expressions, formulas, symbols or traffic signs – that the other person has to translate into meaning. Semiotics is the study of signs; it is a cross-section of sciences from the disciplines of psychology, philosophy, sociology, linguistics, computer science, design, art and mathematics. The bottom line is: we find signs everywhere we come across culture rather than nature.

The key points in brief:

- Some signs – the swastika, a traffic light, the Nike swoosh – are easy to spot and more legible than words. We see them and understand what is meant. A story, a rating, a command or a message springs to mind.
- Perception in most people proceeds from image to text. We remember drawings better than words, recognize patterns in representations more than in sentences.
- Some of the most important semioticians believe that all the following are signs: a Rolls-Royce in front of the door, a blue sky, a hundred-dollar note, open shoelaces, a half-empty or half-full glass of water, a magic formula, a traffic jam on the motorway, a sunset. Nothing can be perceived merely as what it is. It will always (have to) be interpreted by the viewer as a sign of something.

'The visual is like the political: everyone thinks they understand something about it, and to an extent this is true.' So says the German Professor of Mass Communication, Marion G. Müller. She makes an important point about the design of signs and symbols: they are complex but need to be comprehensible, otherwise there can be no communication.

Most people understand complicated matter better through images than in words. We remember pictures better than text and are more likely to recognize patterns in images than in sentences.

40 Euphemism

How we obfuscat

DYSPHEMISM

Ministry of War

Mi

D

with language

EUPHEMISM

ry of
nce

Ministry of
Peace

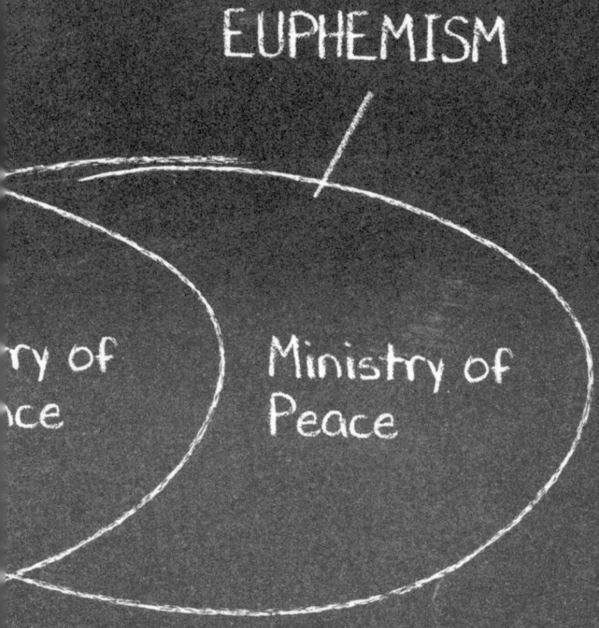

How we obfuscate with language

Speaking in euphemisms is a form of linguistic whitewashing. Governments prefer to speak of 'enhanced interrogation methods' rather than torture. The company spokesman will not say that staff are being dismissed, but that the company is 'restructuring'. Products are 'a bargain', not cheap. If we tell a lie we are simply 'stretching the truth'. And when we are broke, we can give it the fancy expression 'negative cash flow'. The opposite of a euphemism – when you give something a negative meaning – is called a dysphemism: someone with strong political views will immediately become an 'extremist'.

Euphemisms are the stealth bombers of rhetoric. At first glance they are not visible, but their attacks are insidious: by the time you become aware of them, the damage is already done. The Nazis loved euphemisms: 'land consolidation' instead of expulsion, 'labour camp' instead of concentration camp, 'special action' instead of killing.

Euphemisms crop up in almost all political and corporate communications; for example, a town hall meeting might suggest a friendly local gathering where everyone can contribute, but in fact the CEO just wants to get a particular message across. Downsizing suggests a sort of inevitability to making a company somewhat cosier in size without mentioning job cuts.

Euphemisms are the mother tongue of manipulation. As a rule of thumb, if someone doesn't use straight language, don't act straight away – pause before acting.

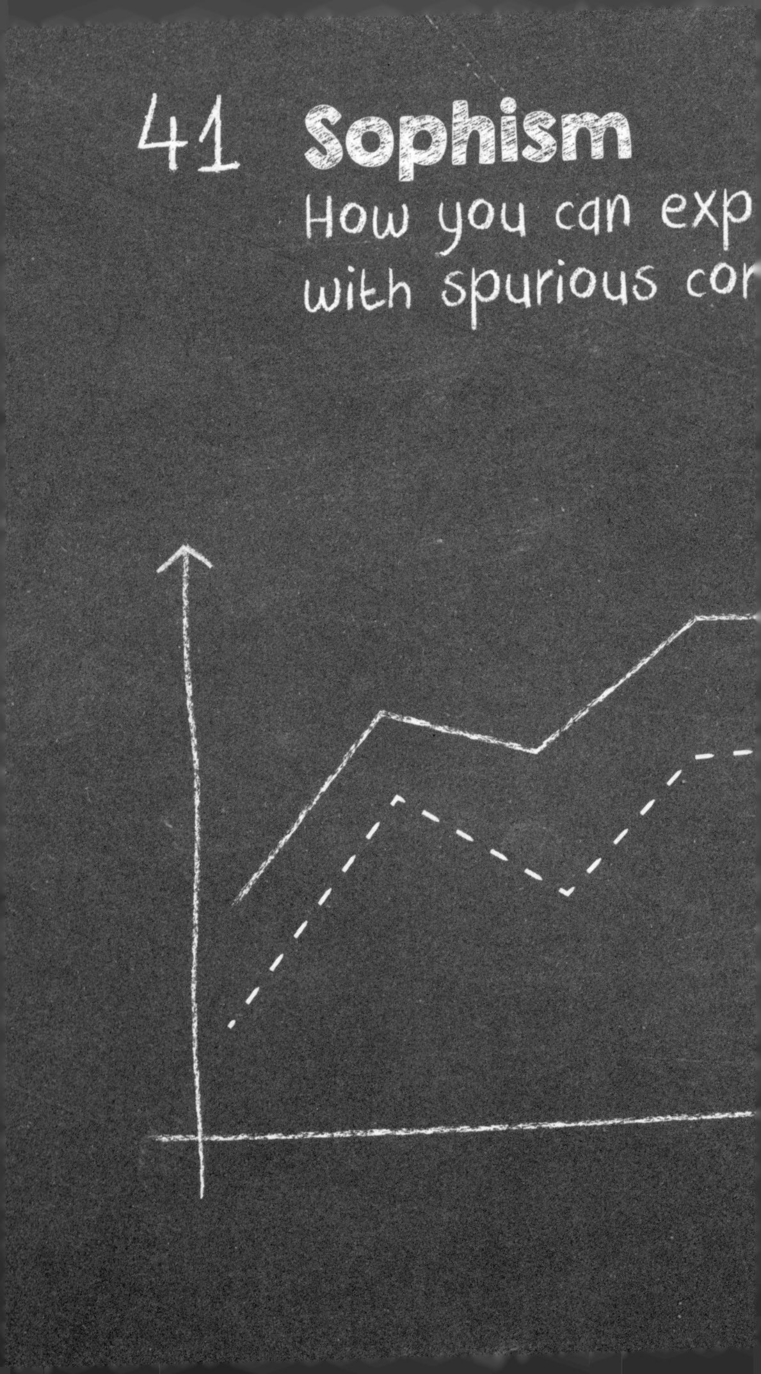
41 Sophism
How you can exp
with spurious cor

n practically anything
ations

Roger Federer's position
in the world ranking

Incidence of twin
births in Switzerland

How you can explain practically anything with spurious correlations

In Ancient Greece, debate was central to the forming of opinions. A distinction between good and bad reasoning was made:

- **Good reasoning** aims to convince, but it also lets itself be convinced. Simply put, it is the search for truth.
- **Bad reasoning** has no interest in the truth; it is simply about wanting to be right.

Plato called bad reasoning 'sophistic'. The Sophists claimed to be able to justify any position through reasoning and logic. They aimed at defeating their opponents in debates using rhetorical strategies (see 'Theory of Rhetoric', p. 18) and logical arguments. The Sophists were unpopular, despised and – successful.

A well-known example is that of Euathlus, who was educated in sophistry by Protagoras. They made an agreement that Euathlus would only have to pay for his instruction after he won his first lawsuit. But after his education Euathlus took up a different profession. Therefore he did not conduct any lawsuits, could not win any, and argued that he did not have to pay for his instruction. Subsequently, Protagoras sued him and argued sophistically: 'Euathlus will pay: if he wins the case, he will have to pay according to the original agreement, and if he loses, the court will order him to pay.' Euathlus, Protagoras' best-trained Sophist, replied: 'I will not have to pay on any account: because if I lose the case I do not have to pay according to the original agreement, and if I win,

I will owe you nothing according to the verdict.' It is an ingenious, logical argument, but also a deliberately induced fallacy – a sophism.

Now, you should not think that sophism died out with the Ancient Greeks. On the contrary: it still exists and is in excellent health! Modern instances of sophism are spurious relationships: 'In spring, storks return from the south. In spring the number of births demonstrably increases. The two things must be linked!' No. The two statements correlate, but are not causal. What's more, they have nothing to do with each other.

'Most of you will have heard the maxim "Correlation does not imply causation." Just because two variables have a statistical relationship with each other does not mean that one is responsible for the other. For instance, ice cream sales and forest fires are correlated because both occur more often in the summer heat. But there is no causation; you don't set a patch of the Montana brush on fire when you buy a pint of Häagen-Dazs.'

Nate Silver

42 The Cultivat

How the media co

Time that w
in our filte

on Theory

oborates our opinions

George Gerbner·Larry Gross

spend

bubble

Openness to
other opinions

How the media corroborates our opinions

One of the most frequently cited communication theories is George Gerbner's Cultivation Theory from 1976, which claims that people who watch a lot of television are more likely to 'cultivate' the belief that reality corresponds with what they are seeing on TV. He argued that watching a lot of television changes our perception of reality and causes anxiety.

The mass media – in the past film and TV, nowadays mostly games and the Internet – confronts us with an exaggerated, stylized world. According to Gerbner, those who consume a lot of media start to see the real world in the way it is stylized on screen. Some examples: in everyday life we rarely see a policeman with a drawn gun; in a crime drama, however, it is standard. In reality we rarely see violence; on screen we see it all the time. According to Gerbner, if we consume these kinds of on-screen images over a long period of time, our perception of reality changes and we begin to internalize it. Even if we don't actually see any violence, we start to *believe* the world is a violent place. And the more violent and frightening images we see, the more anxious we become in our everyday lives.

So the media influences us. But to what extent? Does it mean, for example, that excessively playing FPS (First Person Shooter) games will cause the player to go on a killing spree? No, the media does not form our opinions and beliefs, but it does reinforce them. So somebody who already has violent fantasies will find affirmation for them online. But somebody who coexists peacefully with others will not turn into a serial killer by watching violent films several nights in a row.

It is important to remember that we prefer to watch things we enjoy – as is demonstrated most clearly by the filter-bubble effect: on the Internet, algorithms try to predict what information we will be looking for based on our interests and opinions. That way there is little chance of being convinced by a different opinion, because we are unlikely to be 'served' any alternative views. When it comes to decision making this kind of self-confirming information proves a huge risk, as explained in the chapter on 'Groupthink' (p. 34).

The Cultivation Theory has been criticized for its lack of complexity. Viewers are regarded as passive and easy to manipulate. If you are interested in the opposite view, take a look at 'The Encoding/Decoding Model' (p. 156).

If you like apples and spend hours watching a TV programme about pears, you won't suddenly prefer pears afterwards. But if you already like pears and spend hours watching a programme about pears, you will like pears even more afterwards.

43 The Standp

What opinion has

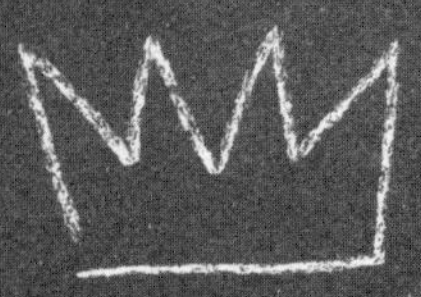

The more powerful
you are...

nt Theory

o do with power

Sandra Harding

...the more convinced you are that your opinion is objective

What opinion has to do with power

Everyone has a voice, but not everyone is heard. The voices that prevail are called 'hegemonic'. The creation of hegemony has little to do with democracy and everything to do with power. It is not a question of who has something legitimate or important to say, but always of who has sufficient resources and influence in a society to define their opinion as legitimate or important. The hegemonic perspective is considered neutral. Anything that deviates from it is seen as an exception and ascribed to others. The hegemonic view claims not to represent a specific point of view, position or life experience, but rather to represent things as simply 'the way they are'.

An example: the media in the Western world is dominated by white male journalists. Nevertheless, the news never announces: 'Today you will hear the news from a white male perspective.' 'White' and 'male' are not explicitly named; they are regarded as general, neutral and non-specific. Another example: if a married couple are heterosexual, their sexual orientation isn't mentioned; if they are homosexual it is.

The question of hegemonic voices is associated with the concept of which truths prevail. Here we come to the Standpoint Theory, whose most important proponents are Donna Haraway and Sandra Harding. They maintain that a voice – or standpoint – cannot be objective or neutral, or exist outside a specific social context. Here is an example: in science – and in children's books to the present day – the idea that prehistoric people hunted mammoths was long considered to be fact. Prehistoric people, or, more concretely, prehistoric men, set off on dangerous mammoth-hunting expeditions. But in fact this image was created in the nineteenth century at a time when hunting was no longer essential for survival, but was simply a status symbol. In their interpretations of prehistory, archaeologists neglected unspectacular types of food procurement such as gathering berries and roots, or trapping small animals.

This is not to say that men did not sometimes slay a mammoth. But it distorts the fact that they mainly collected berries. Here, the historians were not objective, but confirmed the stereotype of men as brave fighters, warriors and family breadwinners, as if this were a law of nature. Bottom line: if you believe that you hold an objective opinion, ask yourself what other points of view were excluded so that yours could prevail.

If you want to make sure that every voice in the room is heard, you can ask your team not to express their opinion about a given topic, but rather brainstorm different possible opinions. That way sooner or later even the unheard voices will appear on the flipchart and once they are up there, they can be discussed.

CONCLUSION

44 The Peak-E

What we rememb

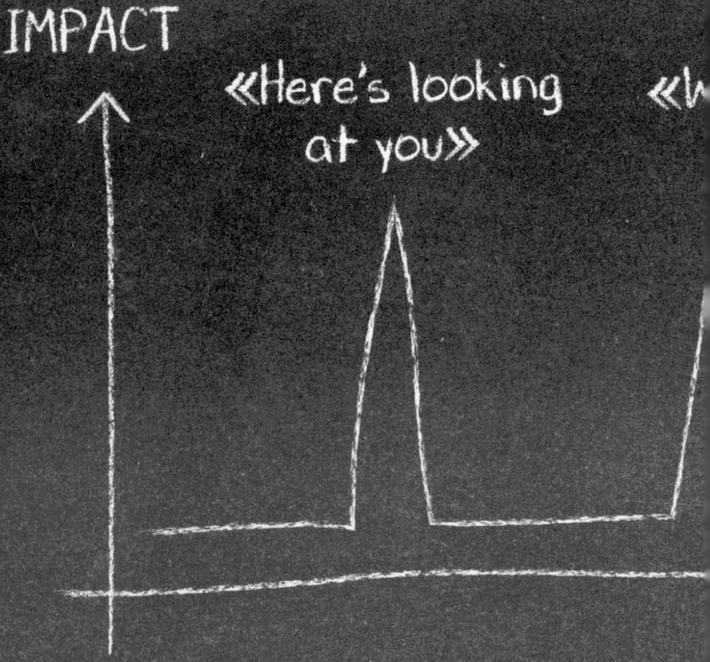

IMPACT

«Here's looking at you»

«W

d Rule

from a Conversation

Daniel Kahneman et al.

l always have Paris»

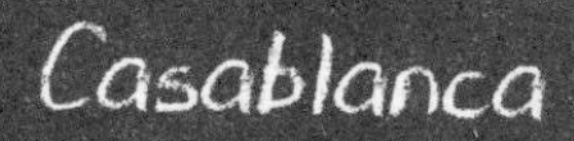

What we remember from a conversation

Here's a question: how do we know if a presentation, a job interview or a date went well?

We usually have a good hunch – but do we really know? Assessing a date would involve some pretty complicated number crunching: we'd have to calculate how we felt, how the other person felt, what we had expected and so on. An impossible task.

It turns out our mind solves this problem by using a surprisingly simple strategy, as Laurie Santos from Yale University explains brilliantly in a lecture: when we remember something we ignore most of it. Actually we make an assessment based only on two parts of the experience:

1. **The peak** – i.e. the part of the experience that was most extreme (either pleasant or unpleasant).
2. **The end** – i.e. whether it got better or worse at the end. (This is important: even a small improvement can make the date seem like an OK experience, whereas a poor ending will ruin an otherwise great evening).

This is the Peak–End Rule, devised in a 1993 study by the Nobel laureate Daniel Kahneman and his colleagues.

How can we use this in our life?

The Peak–End Rule gives us some hints about how to make an experience special:

We often obsess about what kind of first impression we make on people, fearing that people might judge us based only on our outward appearance or first sentences. This thinking is based on the famous notion of 'You only have one chance to make a first impression.' Though this holds true – the first thing we hear about someone influences our judgement of that person, the first price we are quoted forms the basis for the negotiation; it is the anchor effect – maybe we should start obsessing about something else: there might be only one chance to make a *lasting* impression. That lasting impression is not necessarily the first impression, but rather the last one. (That is, by the way, the reason why we binge-watch TV shows: by ending on a cliffhanger they have perfected the Peak-End Rule.)

So when it comes to communication, it is of course important how we start a meeting, how we set the tone, how we break the ice. But, according to Kahneman's work, maybe we should start focusing on how we want to end the whole damned thing.

'I don't care about opening sentences. All I care about is the last sentence. It's the sentence the reader will go to bed with.'

Elfriede Jelinek

Sources

Active Listening: Carl R. Rogers, *Counseling and Psychotherapy*, Houghton Mifflin, Boston, 1942; Celeste Headlee, '10 Ways to Have a Better Conversation', www.ted.com/talks/celeste-headlee-10-ways-to-have-a-better-conversation

Boss Talk: Warren Bennis, *On Becoming a Leader*, Basic Books, New York, 1989

Cooperative Principle: Paul Grice, *Studies in the Way of Words*, Harvard University Press, Cambridge, Mass., 1989

Cultivation Theory: George Gerbner and Larry Gross, 'Living With Television: The Violence Profile', *Journal of Communication*, Vol. 26, No. 2, 1976

Encoding/Decoding Model: Stuart Hall (ed.), *Culture, Media, Language*, Routledge/University of Birmingham, London, 1992

Euphemisms: Malcolm Kushner, *Public Speaking for Dummies*, 2nd edn, John Wiley, Hoboken, 2004

Expectancy Violations Theory: J. K. Burgoon and J. Hale, 'Nonverbal Expectancy Violations: Model Elaboration and Application to Immediacy Behaviors', *Communication Monographs*, Vol. 55, No. 1, 1988, pp. 58–79

Feedback Method: D. L. Cooperrider and D. Whitney, *Appreciative Inquiry: A Positive Revolution in Change*, Berrett-Koehler, San Francisco, 2005

FoMO Phenomenon: A. K. Przybylski, K. Murayama, C. R. DeHaan and V. Gladwell, 'Motivational, Emotional, and Behavioral Correlates of Fear of Missing Out', *Computers in Human Behavior*, No. 29, July 2013

Framing Effect: Erving Goffman, *The Presentation of Self in Everyday Life*, Doubleday, New York/Penguin Books, Harmondsworth, 1959

Game Theory: Erwin Amann, *Spieltheorie für Dummies* [*Game Theory for Dummies*], Wiley, Weinheim, 2012

Groupthink: Irving L. Janis, *Groupthink: Psychological Studies of Policy Decisions and Fiascoes*, 2nd edn, Houghton Mifflin, Boston, 1982

Iceberg Model: Floyd L. Ruch and Philip G. Zimbardo, *Psychology and Life*, 10th edn, Scott, Foresman, Glenview, 1979

Intercultural Communication: Richard D. Lewis, *When Cultures Collide: Leading Across Cultures*, 3rd edn, Nicholas Brealey, Boston, 2007

Lasswell's Communication Model: Harold D. Lasswell, 'The Structure and Function of Communication in Society' (1948), in W. Schramm (ed.), *Mass Communications*, 2nd edn, University of Illinois Press, Urbana, 1960

***L'Esprit de l'escalier*:** William Lewis Hertslet, *Der Treppenwitz der Weltgeschichte: Geschichtliche Irrtümer, Entstellungen und Erfindungen* (1882), BiblioLife, 2008

McLuhan's Media Theory: Marshall McLuhan, *Understanding Media: The Extensions of Man*, McGraw-Hill, New York/Routledge & Kegan Paul, London, 1964

Nonviolent Communication: Marshall B. Rosenberg, *Nonviolent Communication: A Language of Life*, 3rd edn, PuddleDancer Press, Encinitas, 2015

Parenting Tips: Tips from Jessica Hagy (diagram), Remo Largo, Jesper Juul, Brett R. Kuhn, Joe Borgenicht and Gina Ford

Power Method: Robert Greene, *The 48 Laws of Power*, Viking Penguin, New York, 1998

Principled Negotiation: Roger Fisher, William L. Ury and Bruce M. Patton (ed.), *Getting to Yes: Negotiating Agreement without Giving In*, Houghton Mifflin, Boston, 1991

Proust's Questionnaire: William C. Carter and Henry-Jean Servat, *The Proust Questionnaire*, Assouline, New York, 2005

Rules of Meetings: C. Northcote Parkinson, *Parkinson's Law, and Other Studies in Administration*, Ballantine, New York, 1957

Salami Tactic: Mária Palasik, *Chess Game for Democracy: Hungary between East and West, 1944–1947*, McGill-Queen's University Press, Montreal, 2011

Schulz von Thun's Communication Model: Friedemann Schulz von Thun, *Miteinander Reden 1: Störungen und Klärungen*, Rowohlt, Reinbek, 1981

Second-Order Observation: Niklas Luhmann, *Die Kunst der Gesellschaft* [*Art as a Social System*], Suhrkamp, Frankfurt am Main, 1997

Self-Talk: Steven G. Rogelberg et al., 'The Executive Mind: Leader Self-Talk, Effectiveness and Strain', *Journal of Managerial Psychology*, Vol. 28, No. 2, 2013, pp. 183–201

Six Principles of Persuasion: Robert Cialdini, *Influence: The Psychology of Persuasion*, Collins, New York, 2007

Six-Word Rule: Larry Smith, *Not Quite What I was Planning: Six-Word Memoirs by Writers Famous and Obscure*, Harper, New York, 2008

Small Talk: Gretchen Rubin, *The Happiness Project*, HarperCollins, New York, 2009

Social Judgement Theory: Muzafer Sherif and Carl Hovland, *Social Judgment: Assimilation and Contrast Effects in Communication and Attitude Change*, Yale University Press, New Haven/London, 1961

Sophism: Bertrand Russell, *A History of Western Philosophy* (1946), Routledge, London, 2004

Sorry Matrix: Roy J. Lewicki, Beth Polin and Robert B. Lount Jr, 'An Exploration of the Structure of Effective Apologies', *Negotiation and Conflict Management Research*, Vol. 9, Issue 2, May 2016, pp. 177–96

Speech Act Theory: J. L. Austin, *How to Do Things with Words* (William James Lectures, 1955), Harvard University Press, Cambridge, Mass./Clarendon Press, Oxford, 1962

Spiral of Silence: Elisabeth Noelle-Neumann, *The Spiral of Silence: Public Opinion – Our Social Skin*, University of Chicago Press, Chicago/London, 1984

Standpoint Theory: Sandra Harding (ed.), *The Feminist Standpoint Theory Reader: Intellectual and Political Controversies*, Routledge, New York/London, 2004

Storytelling: Walter Fisher, 'Narrative Paradigm', in Em Griffin, Andrew Ledbetter and Glenn Sparks (eds), *A First Look at Communication Theory*, 9th edn, McGraw-Hill, New York, 2014, Ch. 24, pp. 303–13; William Labov, 'Some Further Steps in Narrative Analysis', *The Journal of Narrative and Life History*, No. 7, Issue 1–4, 1997, pp. 395–415

Theory of Rhetoric: Aristotle (trans. Franz G. Sieveke), *Rhetorik*, Wilhelm Fink, Paderborn, 2010

Transactional Analysis: Eric Berne, *Transactional Analysis in Psychotherapy: A Systematic Individual and Social Psychiatry*, Castle, New York, 1961

Uses and Gratifications Theory: Elihu Katz, 'Uses and Gratifications', in Em Griffin, Andrew Ledbetter and Glenn Sparks (eds), *A First Look at Communication Theory*, 9th edn, McGraw-Hill, New York, 2014, Ch. 28, pp. 353–62

Visual Communication: Roland Barthes, *Mythologies*, Cape, London, 1972

Watzlawick's Axiom Theory: Paul Watzlawick, Janet Beavin Bavelas and Don D. Jackson, *Pragmatics of Human Communication: A Study of Interactional Patterns, Pathologies and Paradoxes*, W. W. Norton, New York/London, 2011

White Lies: Sanjiv Erat and Uri Gneezy, 'White Lies', *Management Science*, Vol. 58, No. 4, 2012, pp. 723–33

Thanks

We are very grateful to the following people who were involved in the making of this book: Rebecca De Bautista (for the graphic design), Peter Haag (for making it possible), Jessica Hagy (for the Solar System Model), Marlene Iseli (for advice on linguistics), Juri Jacquemet (ici c'est Bienne!), Angelina Keller (for staying on the ball), Jan-Dirk Kemming (for intelligent advice), Julian Lambertin (for generously sharing his knowledge), Benno Maggi (for sparring), Ondine Riesen (for actively listening), Christian Rohner (for crystal-clear communication), Gretchen Rubin (for small-talk tips), Ueli Schenk (for his detailed as well as inspiring feedback), Sara Schindler (for proofreading), Franziska Schutzbach (for gender-sensitive language and always moving the conversation forward), Marcelo Aragón Taravella (for the inner team), Detlef Vögeli (for intelligent feedback), Sven Weber (for the illustrations).

We would particularly like to thank everyone at the Museum of Communication, Bern, Switzerland, for a great collaboration and for believing in us.

The Authors

Mikael Krogerus, born in 1976, is an editor at *Das Magazin*. He has also worked for the youth TV show *Chat the Planet* in New York and for the NZZ *Folio* in Zurich.

Roman Tschäppeler, born in 1978, founded his studio 'guzo' in 2003, where he develops and produces films, campaigns and multimedia projects.

Mikael and Roman are both graduates of Kaospilot business school in Denmark and are also authors of the international bestseller *The Decision Book* and three other books that explain complex theories using simple diagrams. They regularly give keynote speeches and lectures in which they present their findings using only an old school blackboard.

rtmk.ch

Other books by the authors
The Decision Book
The Change Book
The Test Book
The Question Book

The Communication Book

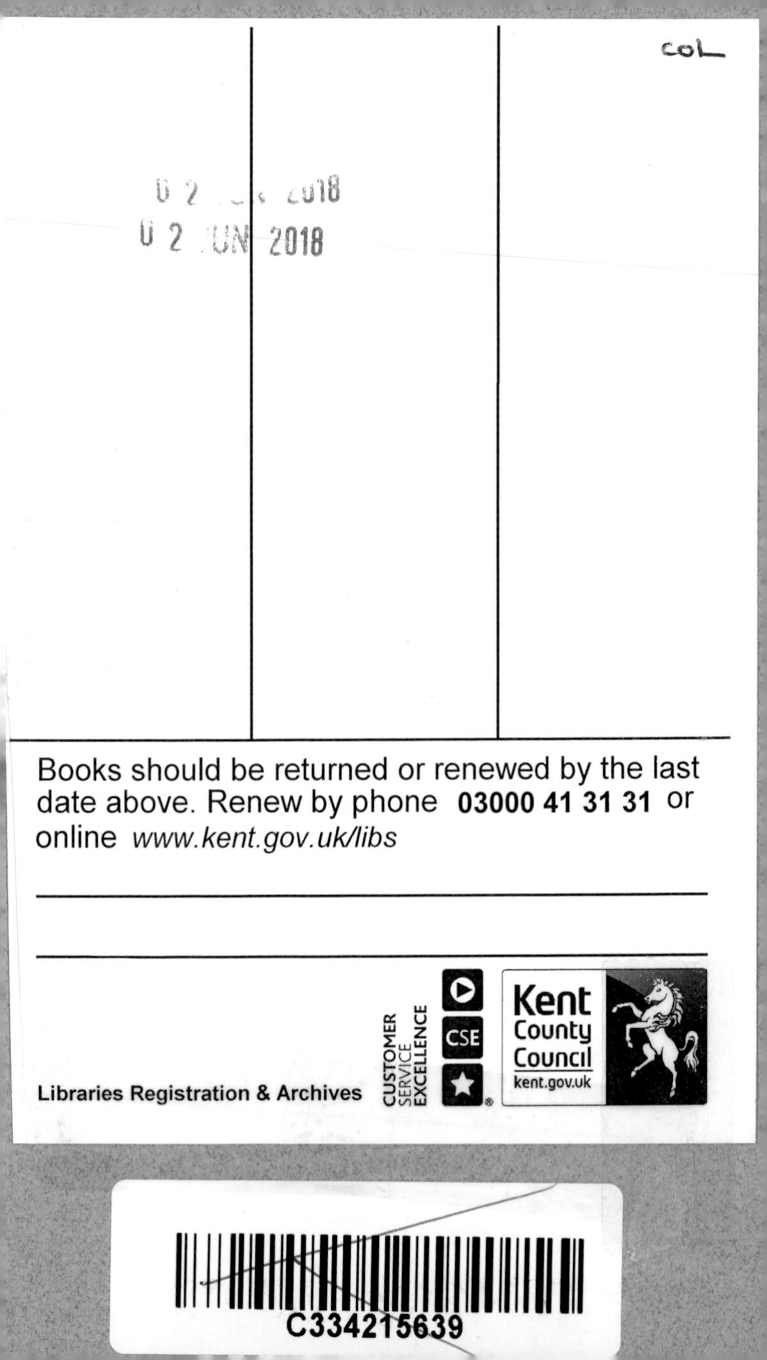